The impeachment of
Michael de la Pole
Earl of Suffolk
in 1386

The impeachment of
Michael de la Pole
Earl of Suffolk
in 1386
in the context of the
reign of Richard II

J. S. ROSKELL

MANCHESTER
UNIVERSITY PRESS

Published by
Manchester University Press
Oxford Road, Manchester M13 9PL, U.K.
51 Washington Street, Dover, N.H. 03820, U.S.A.

British Library
cataloguing in publication data
Roskell, J.S.
    The impeachment of Michael de la Pole,
    Earl of Suffolk in 1386.
    1. Suffolk, Michael de la Pole. *Earl of*
    2. Impeachment—England
    I. Title
    354.4103′6   JF323

    ISBN 0–7190–0963–4

Library of Congress
cataloging in publication data
Roskell, John Smith.
    The impeachment of Michael de la Pole, Earl of
Suffolk in 1386.
    Bibliography:
    Includes index.
    1. Suffolk, Michael de la Pole, Earl of, 1330?–1389.
    2. Trials (Impeachment)—England. I. Title.
KD7105.5.R67   1984   347.41′016   83–10608
ISBN 0–7190–0963–4   344.10716

Phototypeset by Wilmaset, Birkenhead, Merseyside
Printed in Great Britain
by Butler & Tanner Ltd, Frome and London

Contents

Acknowledgments

I wish to thank Dr R. G. Davies, Dr P. McNiven, and Professor E. L. G. Stones, all of whom took pains to read what I had at first vainly imagined might be my finished text. In their different ways they criticised it, but in each case so constructively as to persuade me to seek publication. For their help and encouragement I offer them my very hearty thanks.

List of abbreviations

B.I.H.R.	Bulletin of the Institute of Historical Research
C.Charter R.	*Calendar of Charter Rolls*
C.C.R.	*Calendar of Close Rolls*
C.F.R.	*Calendar of Fine Rolls*
Cal.Inqs.p.m.	*Calendar of Inquisitions post mortem*
C.P.R.	*Calendar of Patent Rolls*
D.N.B.	*Dictionary of National Biography*
E.H.R.	*The English Historical Review*
Foedera	Thomas Rymer, *Foedera, Conventiones, etc.*, London, 1704–1735
P.R.O.	Public Record Office
R.S.	Rolls Series
Rot. Parl.	*Rotuli Parliamentorum*, Record Commission, 1767–1777
T.R.H.S.	*Transactions of the Royal Historical Society*

Introduction

Historians have always recognised the general importance of the 'Wonderful Parliament' of 1386 for subsequent developments in the reign of Richard II: 'with it', rightly said William Stubbs, 'the clearer and more dramatic action of the reign begins'.[1] Indeed, there was even soon to emerge a more serious crisis, one attended by much more violent action, culminating in the 'Merciless Parliament' of 1388. One notable factor leading to *this* crisis was the unease, not to say desperation, felt by the king's aristocratic opponents and others, created by the questionnaire put to the royal judges in the summer of 1387 and by the answers they made to it, answers which 'represented a more explicit statement than any which had yet been articulated in England of the right of the monarch to select his own ministers and advisers without interference, to summon and dissolve parliament when he chose, to prescribe the business with which parliament should be concerned, and to be the final unquestioned executor of national policy', and which 'left no ambiguity on the score of the peril of tampering with the prerogative' (R. H. Jones).[2] That questionnaire referred back directly to the doings of the 1386 parliament, where Lords and Commons had made common cause in their opposition to Richard's government. Initially, they had gone so far as to allow the king to be threatened with deposition if, deliberately absenting himself from parliament in order to prevent the dismissal and impeachment of his chancellor, Michael de la Pole, he did not return and take part; then, when Richard had complied with their demand and also dismissed the chancellor, they had proceeded to the latter's impeachment, trial and condemnation; and, finally, they had established a council of parliament's choosing endowed with statutory powers to take over the conduct of government and administration. What the judges emphatically upheld was Richard's objection on principle to all the acts of the 1386 parliament, including the judgment upon De la Pole's impeachment, which, they opined, had been erroneous and was revocable. This particular answer of the judges supplemented their ruling on impeachments in general, which, since the removal of all royal officials was for the king's prerogatival action alone, ought never to be undertaken by the Lords and Commons 'absque voluntate Regis', that is, without royal permission freely given. Whether or not modern historians of the period have differed as to the immediate significance of De la Pole's impeachment, political or otherwise, they have all been obliged to comment.

Curiously, however, consideration of the actual content of the charges brought against the deposed chancellor has been remarkably exiguous. T. F. T. Plucknett, in a presidential address to the Royal Historical Society (1952) entitled 'State Trials under Richard II',[3] dealt with De la Pole's impeachment, but he was naturally concerned only to discuss it as a form of criminal proceeding. In fact, only two of the seven accusations made by the Commons have ever been considered in anything like adequate detail: article VII of the impeachment, touching De la Pole's responsibility for the final failure of the rebellion of the Flemish communes with the loss of Ghent to the French in 1385, discussed by N. B. Lewis in 1927;[4] and article II, touching De la Pole's failure to carry out the important ordinance embodying proposals for greater governmental financial stringency, as devised by a committee of lords set up for the purpose in the parliament of 1385, dealt with by J. J. N. Palmer in 1969[5] and again in 1971.[6] The conclusion arrived at by Lewis was that the seventh charge was ill-founded, whereas Palmer established that the second was well-founded. The two charges were alike in two respects: they were both concerned with De la Pole's official conduct as chancellor; and De la Pole, in answering to each of them, affirmed that he was only partly responsible for what had occurred, meaning that responsibility had been shared by fellow members of the royal Council. The same is true, in both respects, of the charge contained in article III, in which the Commons objected that their terms for the appropriation of taxes granted in 1385 had been ignored. And then there was the charge, contained in article VI, concerning unreasonable grants of charters, particularly a charter conferring a special franchise upon Dover castle, again a charge of negligence attributable to De la Pole as chancellor, but negligence for which now the blame could not be shared, and which, although he made excuses, he admitted to be true. These third and sixth articles have never been investigated in detail. Nor has any one of the other three charges of the impeachment, those contained in articles I, IV and V, which may be set apart from the rest since they relate to peculation, that is, to De la Pole's exploitation of his custody of the great seal for personal advantage. It is my intention to investigate the impeachment as a whole: to annotate all seven charges individually and, on this basis, assess their significance in general.

That historians, apart from the two honourable exceptions noted, have not undertaken such a detailed examination, may be because they have been "put off" or dissuaded by the opinions of their predecessors, opinions which, sometimes based on possibly no more than a cursory enquiry into the charges, have been even contemptuously dismissive of their importance. Dr Palmer, when introducing his paper on article II, was able to say that 'despite the importance of the event, the articles of accusation . . . have been unanimously labelled irrelevant, trivial, or malicious', and he briefly quoted in support of this statement the synonyms employed by T. F. Tout, N. B. Lewis, and M. V. Clarke, all of them specialists in fourteenth century English history. Given the 'Whig interpretation' of so much of our constitutional and political history and, in particular, the unpopularity of Richard II, that 'autocrat on principle' (V. H. Galbraith), it is perhaps odd that

De la Pole, Richard's faithful minister, should have had "a good press". But such is the case. There is, of course, much to be said for the idea that it was Richard, his court party and his whole government that were really under attack in 1386, and not only De la Pole's policy as chancellor and his personal conduct when in office, the highest placed official and most influential member of the royal administration though he was. Tout and James Tait shared this view: in his biography of De la Pole in *The Dictionary of National Biography* (1896), Tout stated that 'the only real complaint against the fallen minister was his attachment to an unpopular policy';[7] and Tait, in his biography of Richard II (*ibid.*, 1896) evidently felt that he need say no more of De la Pole's impeachment than that 'the charges . . . show he was made the scapegoat of Richard's policy'.[8] Charles Oman (1906) took the same line: 'the accusations . . . were intended to strike the king'.[9] So did J. H. Ramsay (1913): 'the king was the offender, but he could only be attacked through his ministers, however guiltless they might be'.[10] Likewise May McKisack (1959): 'public opinion, no less than private animosities, demanded a scapegoat; and the most eligible victim was the chancellor, Suffolk'.[11] But if, as B. L. Manning (1932) too believed, 'the prosecution was a political move',[12] this was only because the charges brought by the Commons against De la Pole were regarded by these, and other, historians as lacking in inherent seriousness: trumped-up.

The catalogue of such opinions is long, but perhaps not uninteresting in itself, if only as showing how, by reiteration, opinions are liable to acquire firm acceptance. But first as to views upon the impeachment as a whole. Here, we need hardly go back beyond David Hume (1762): 'nothing can prove more fully the innocence of Suffolk than the frivolousness of the articles which his enemies, in the present plenitude of their power, thought proper to object against him'.[13] Henry Hallam (1818) went not far short of this rejection: the charges, 'without being wholly frivolous, were not so weighty as the clamour of the commons might have led us to expect'.[14] Tout was more downright, remarking (1896) upon 'the paltry character of the charges', and upon De la Pole's offences as 'insignificant' (1896),[15] 'neither heinous nor well substantiated (1928)'.[16] N. B. Lewis (1927) found the charges 'trivial or unfounded', 'merely pretexts for dismissing the chief minister of an unpopular king'.[17] Anthony Steel (1941) went so far as to say that, even at the time, 'the whole episode appeared . . . an open travesty of justice'.[18] Moreover, even if some historians were circumspect enough to distinguish between, on the one hand, the allegations that De la Pole had failed to fulfil his cancellarial duties and, on the other, those which reflected upon his personal probity while in office, the general tenor of their remarks was much the same. Referring to the charges of chicanery, Thomas Carte (1750) said that they 'will scarce appear worthy of so extraordinary a prosecution', and that the sentence was one which De la Pole 'had not merited'.[19] William Stubbs (1880) was similarly firm in De la Pole's defence: 'it is quite clear that in his administrative capacity he was equitably entitled to acquittal';[20] and he was also ready to exonerate, or at least to excuse him on the charges of peculation—'a charge of malversation would easily be believed when so much malversation was known to exist, and the imputation so liberally made'.[21] Tout was eventually (1928) to use the same plea: 'the charges proved hardly suggested more than the normal medieval laxity in the acceptance of presents and grants'.[22] S. Armitage-Smith (1904) made only a snap judgment: the charge of malversation was 'baseless', and De la Pole 'disproved' it.[23] J. F. Baldwin (1913) was similarly perfunctory: 'some of the accusations [those relating to De la Pole's official negligence] were preposterous certainly, and others [those relating to his dishonesty] were lacking in proof'.[24] M. V. Clarke (1928) was more expansive but, having noted that 'the general charges . . . could not be pressed', did not then hesitate to say that 'the impeachment . . . degenerated into three badly sustained and trivial charges, behind which motives of malice or private interest may be suspected', charges to which De la Pole made 'an able defence'.[25] These same three charges, about the frauds upon which De la Pole was convicted, were in A. Steel's opinion only 'technicalities'.[26] The view of this part of the case held by May McKisack (1959) was that it was 'manifestly weak'.[27] R. H. Jones (1968) took much the same line: 'The personal charges were petty in nature . . . The most that could be established was that the chancellor had been guilty of sharp but not dishonest business practices in one instance' (presumably the charge in article V regarding St. Anthony's Hospital); and in respect of the accusations of official misconduct, he found them 'even less substantial'.[28] Even allowing for J. E. A. Jolliffe's brief allusion to the impeachment (1937)—'The clearest charges were those of misuse of office to make private profit'[29]—and the irresolute opinion of T. F. T. Plucknett (1946)—'There is reason to believe that Suffolk was as much "sinned against as sinning" '[30]—well might Dr Palmer have questioned whether 'in the face of such unanimity, further enquiry might seem so much wasted effort'.[31]

I propose to deal with the articles of the impeachment, not in the order in which they are recorded in the roll of the parliament of 1386, but rather as befits the nature of the content of the charges and of the Lords' several judgments upon them. My first concern, therefore, will be to examine articles 2, 3 and 7, all of which concern Michael de la Pole's alleged failure, as chancellor, to implement certain decisions taken by the parliament of 1385, charges regarding which he was able to plead that if he himself had been at all negligent, he was not alone to blame, his responsibility having been one shared by fellow ministers and other members of the royal Council, a plea which the Lords accepted as reasonable. I shall then enquire into article 6, which, although protesting in general terms against Michael's allowance of pardons of felonies and grants of charters, drew attention specifically to a charter granting franchises to Dover castle, Michael's plea in this instance being that he was innocent of ill-intent, that the charter had been supported by a sufficient warrant, and that this and any other objectionable charters were revocable without need for any personal penalty, a plea which again was accepted by the Lords. And then, finally, I shall consider articles 1, 4 and 5, in which the charges related to Michael's exploitation of his office to acquire, by deception, landed property or to benefit himself financially otherwise, all to the detriment of the Crown, his defence in each instance being rejected and an adverse judgment rendered by the Lords.

Notes

1 William Stubbs, *The Constitutional History of England* (Library Edition, Oxford, 1880), II, 510.
2 R. H. Jones, *The Royal Policy of Richard II: Absolutism in the Later Middle Ages* (Oxford, 1968), 42. And see S. B. Chrimes, 'Richard II's Questions to the Judges, 1387', *Law Quarterly Review*, LXXII (1956), 365–90.
3 *Transactions of the Royal Historical Society*, 5th series, II. 159–71.
4 *E.H.R.*, XLII, 402–7, 'Article VII of the Impeachment of Michael de la Pole in 1386'.
5 *B.I.H.R.*, XLII, 96–9, 'The Impeachment of Michael de la Pole in 1386'.
6 *Speculum*, XLVI, 477–90, 'The Parliament of 1385 and the Constitutional Crisis of 1386'.
7 *D.N.B.*, XVI, 32.
8 Ibid., 1034.
9 Charles Oman, *History of England from the accession of Richard II to the death of Richard III* (1377–1485) (London, 1906), 99.
10 J. H. Ramsay, *The Genesis of Lancaster, 1307–1399* (Oxford, 1913), 236.
11 May McKisack, *The Fourteenth Century, 1307–1399* (Oxford, 1959), 442.
12 *Cambridge Medieval History*, VII (Cambridge, 1932), 469.
13 David Hume, *History of England* (London, 1762) II, 251.
14 Henry Hallam, *View of the State of Europe during the Middle Ages* (London, 1818), II, 274.
15 See note 7.
16 T. F. Tout, *Chapters in the Administrative History of Mediaeval England* (Manchester, 1920–33), III, 413.
17 See note 4.
18 Anthony Steel, *Richard II* (Cambridge, 1941), 123.
19 Thomas Carte, *A General History of England* (London, 1750), 576.
20 Op. cit., vol. II, 518.
21 Ibid., p. 514.

22 Tout, *Chapters*, III, 414.

23 Sydney Armitage-Smith, *John of Gaunt* (London, 1904), 339.

24 J. F. Baldwin, *The King's Council during the Middle Ages* (Oxford, 1913), 127.

25 M. V. Clarke, *Fourteenth Century Studies*, ed. L. S. Sutherland and M. McKisack (Oxford, 1937), 48, 51. (As noted by the editors, Chapter II, the paper entitled 'The Lancastrian Faction and the Wonderful Parliament' was read in July 1928).

26 Op. cit., 123.

27 Op. cit., 445.

28 Op. cit., 32.

29 J. E. A. Jolliffe, *The Constitutional History of Medieval England* (London, 1937), 459.

30 T. P. Taswell-Langmead, *English Constitutional History*, 10th edition by T. F. T. Plucknett (London, 1946), 191 n. (n).

31 *B.I.H.R.*, XLII, 96.

PART I

---

*The context of the
impeachment*

I

The origins of the crisis of 1386

[handwritten annotation: miscalled "Someone misunderstood the chronicler Favent, who was actually referring to Parl. in 1388"]

The events of the 'Wonderful Parliament' of 1386—chiefly, the dismissal from the office of chancellor of England of Michael de la Pole, earl of Suffolk, immediately followed by his impeachment, trial and condemnation, and the establishment thereafter of a parliamentary commission with wide powers, which Richard II opposed but could not prevent—set the political stage for the rest of the king's reign. Those events constituted a crisis. But the crisis had been long developing, and, to put it into perspective, its origins must needs be sought not only in Richard's earlier years, but further back still, in Edward III's reign.

Of all the various concurrent causes involved, the resumption of the French war in 1369 had contributed most to the crisis. For not only did that policy of renewal of war prove financially exacting, a fact which in turn led to frequent and heavy grants of direct taxation, but the policy itself was quite unrelieved in its execution by any firm compensatory success, either military or diplomatic. Failure in a long-drawn-out but frequently intensive effort led to a serious loss of confidence in the government, and, indeed, on the part of the government in itself. Then, too, the way that the royal administration was ordered internally had only made a confused and difficult situation worse; and the general loss of confidence was, of course, exacerbated by royal incapacity—Edward III's decrepitude and moral deterioration, and his successor Richard II's nonage and immaturity of character. Bewilderment, mistrust and discontent came to pervade all ranks of society. So far as the

lower orders were concerned, this came to a head in the
Peasants' Revolt of 1381, a short, sharp spasm of rebellion
which, while it lasted, convulsed whole areas of the countryside
in the south and east, took a quite heavy toll of life in London
and did great damage to property there, seriously affected a
number of other towns up and down England, and resulted in
the murder of the chancellor (Archbishop Sudbury), the
treasurer (Sir Robert Hales), and the chief justice of the King's
Bench (Sir John Cavendish). So far as the nobility and gentry
were concerned, there was general support for the war with
France, and a desire to continue it, a desire which, naturally,
was most potent among those who, involved in campaigns,
would stand to make 'gains of war'. But, in even their ranks,
there was sometimes protest at military incompetence and
inefficiency. There was also uncertainty as to means, notably a
division of opinion over general strategy, and this was especially
the case in the 1380s. Was negotiation or open war to be
preferred, and if the latter, ought France first to be attacked
directly, by renewal of invasion of the land of France itself, or
indirectly, by war waged upon her allies, and if *this* idea were to
prevail, whether against Castile or in Flanders, as well as upon
Scotland? Such confusion and disagreement generated dissen-
sion among the magnates, bitter quarrels between some of them
and members of the king's government, all of which reinforced
a tendency to political intrigue and, occasionally, violent
reaction. Those who were not in control of policy sometimes
only criticised, but at other times resorted to stronger measures
against those who were. And then, too, at the Court there
persisted the usual competition for crown patronage, royal
offices and other benefits, among the nobles who frequented it,
including members of the royal family, not to mention the
lesser courtiers, who, in pursuit of petty personal ambitions,
were so often at odds with one another. With the state of the
royal Household as a whole, there was great public dissatisfaction; and this, as was the case with so much else, found its most
opportune outlet in parliament, especially among the Commons, who were always ready to disapprove of the Household's

costliness, censure its extravagance, and suspect, even (given evidence) inveigh against, its corruption and the malpractices of its officials and servants. In this respect, the demise of Edward III, a king who had become too old, and the accession of Richard II, a king who was then too young, made little, if any, difference: despite the warnings contained in the punishments and reprimands dealt out in the 'Good Parliament' of 1376, and the discovery then made by the Commons of the rôle they could play in impeaching the king's ministers (not least, as on that occasion, the highest officials of the royal Household), the early years of Richard's reign gave rise to scandals hardly less serious than those which had characterised the time of his grandfather's decline. This is not to say that the mere fact of Richard's minority and personal incapacity had not of itself raised serious questions.

The malaise characteristic of the two decades following upon the resumption of the French war in 1369 did not only find an outlet in the adversely critical attitude towards the government so often adopted by the frequent parliaments of the period. Parliament's dissatisfaction prompted it also to make positive efforts to improve the situation. That these efforts came to nothing was to a large extent because of royal incapacity and the lack of firm leadership or direction. But not altogether: if to some extent parliament's efforts were unsuccessful in improving the tone and effectiveness of government and administration, this was because parliament itself was apt to be impatient of its own remedies. Especially was this so when these resulted, for example, in instability in the royal Council (at least in the sense of discontinuity of its membership), and also, at any rate in the earliest years of Richard II's minority, in rapid changes among some of the great officers of state, who naturally, as *ex officio* members of the Council, formed its core and supplied its motive force. The "turnover" among the chancellors, the most important and influential of such officers, was in this connexion quite the most remarkable: between the beginning of Richard II's reign in June 1377 and March 1383, when Michael de la Pole was appointed, there was a succession of seven appoint-

ments to the custody of the great seal (involving six officers).[1]
That by the time of Michael's dismissal in October 1386 his
tenure of office reached back uninterruptedly for three and a
half years was so exceptional as possibly to have counted against
him,[2] especially given the political reasons prompting that
relatively long continuance. Given also parliament's better-
informed awareness in 1386 of his arbitrary conduct of affairs,
and particularly his contempt for its own previous decisions,
any further prolongation of his appointment must have seemed
something to be prevented at all costs. This is not to say,
however, that the main gravamen of the charges preferred
against him in the 'Wonderful Parliament'—that he had
increasingly exploited his office for personal advantage —was
but a pretext for bringing about his dismissal or even justifying
it in retrospect. Ministerial responsibility to parliament for
personal as well as official conduct was what was then at stake,
and no one recognised more clearly that this was a crucial issue
in Michael's dismissal and impeachment than Richard II
himself. There were, however, other considerations involved,
considerations just as deep-seated and important.

Notes

1   For references in this and later pages to appointments of
    chancellors, keepers of the privy seal and treasurers of the
    Exchequer, see *Handbook of British Chronology*, ed. Sir F.
    Maurice Powicke and E. B. Fryde, 2nd edition (London, 1961).
    One of the seven appointments to the chancellorship was to
    replace Adam Houghton on 29 October 1378, by which time the
    bishop was over seventy years old and no doubt feeling the
    burden of his years; and another was occasioned by the murder of
    Archbishop Sudbury on 14 June 1381, during the Peasants'
    Revolt.

2   The last thing I would wish to imply is that frequent change in
    the tenure of the chancellorship was something properly
    desirable in itself. Few would have objected to a longer
    continuance in office by Richard, lord Scrope, who, appointed
    (for the second time in the reign) on 4 December 1381,
    voluntarily discharged himself on 11 July 1382, for Scrope's
    conduct in office was anything but unsound.

II

Politics and parliaments, 1371–86

Despite the strains and stresses of Edward III's reign, which were ultimately a consequence of the war with France, no serious governmental crisis had occurred between 1340–1 and 1371. On each of these two occasions the chancellor and the treasurer, both of them bishops, were dismissed and, in order that such important ministers might be answerable in the royal courts for their offences, replaced by laymen.[1] Moreover, the charge preferred each time was basically the same: remissness in providing adequate administrative support for the war. But whereas in 1340–1 it had been the king himself who, in incriminating his own officials, objected to their claim as churchmen for protection under the canon law, in the 1371 parliament it was the Commons who, for similar reasons, specifically demanded the appointment of laymen. And this was what was done. Indeed, not only was Bishop Wykeham of Winchester then superseded as chancellor by Sir Robert Thorpe (chief justice of the Common Bench), and Bishop Brantingham of Exeter as treasurer by Richard, lord Scrope, but another layman, Nicholas Carew, became keeper of the privy seal. Carew retained office until the king's death; and although the other two did not, their successors (Sir John Knyvet and Sir Robert Assheton) were also laymen, and both stayed in office almost to the end of the reign (until January 1377). Only then were bishops (Adam Houghton of St David's and Henry Wakefield of Worcester) again appointed as chancellor and treasurer. Perhaps another important motive behind the replacement of ecclesiastics in the two topmost offices of state had been to avoid any such tenderness as officials who were bishops might feel towards the clergy, whose financial contributions to national defence were sometimes thought to fall far short of what seemed reasonable. However this may be, the lay ministry of the sort established in 1371 proved no more successful in maintaining the war than its predecessor. Dissatisfaction did not abate.

Apart from failure on the strictly military side following upon the renewal of the French war in 1369, this continuance of dissatisfaction was for two basic reasons. First, although it was only to be expected that, with an increase of legitimate expenditure, direct taxation would be resumed (after being totally in abeyance during the '60s), royal demands—met in 1371 by a tax on parishes (designed to produce £50,000) and in 1373 by two tenths and fifteenths (worth even more)—were to intensify. Second, when in 1376 further grants were necessary, and accordingly parliament was again summoned, there was soon added to the strong suspicion that the proceeds of taxation were being inefficiently used, and opportunities for economy neglected, a sense of outrage resulting from the revelation that officials of the king's own Household and others of the court circle were corruptly exploiting their natural advantage for private monetary gain, all to the detriment of the revenue. In view of the lapse of two and a half years since the last previous parliament, it is hardly surprising that in the 'Good Parliament' of 1376 all the pent-up dissatisfaction with the conduct of the war came to a head, and vented itself in hostile political expression, namely, an eruption of anti-governmental feeling.

Whether some in the Lords, like the earl of March (whose steward, Sir Peter de la Mare, soon emerged as spokesman for the Commons), prompted the Commons to act or, as the Black Prince would seem to have done from his death-bed, merely sympathised with them, it was the Lower House which now took the initiative. Even though repeatedly asked for financial aid, the Commons refused, doing so, general pleas of poverty apart, on the grounds of waste and misuse of previous grants, and because of official corruption resulting in direct financial loss to the Crown. Admittedly, the Commons requested a reconstitution of the king's Council and the dismissal of both chancellor and treasurer; but these demands only *followed* revelations made in the course of the investigation of the misconduct of William, lord Latimer, the king's chamberlain, and of certain London financiers, chief among them Richard Lyons, Latimer's ally, and neither the chancellor nor the treasurer underwent detailed enquiry on the score of *their* behaviour, let alone suffered dismissal. It was the misconduct of Latimer and Lyons that roused the Commons to greatest indignation. The three main charges of which the Commons impeached them[2] were that, contrary to a previous parliamentary decision, they had procured the removal of the Staple from Calais, an action which had served both to annul royal revenue from the Calais Exchange and to shift the burden of maintaining the town's military garrison from the merchants of the Staple to the Crown; that during Lord Scrope's treasurership they had lent 20,000 marks to the Crown, including money of the king's own to which they had official access, and at a rate of interest (50 per cent) which was made to appear all the more exorbitant when certain London merchants offered to lend 15,000 marks quite free of interest[3]; and that, following loans to the Crown made by various prelates and townsmen, they had bought up the Exchequer tallies of repayment by assignment, at discounts which, quite apart from undermining the king's credit as a borrower, had yielded them personally a profit equivalent to their outlay. It was for similarly manipulating Exchequer methods of repayment that the steward of the royal Household, John, lord Neville, Latimer's brother-in-law, was also impeached by the Commons, with the result that he was dismissed from his post and membership of the Council. So, too, of course, had Latimer been, but with his offences considered the more scandalous, the peers had also sentenced him to imprisonment and payment of fine and ransom to the king. However, much of the work of the 'Good Parliament' was soon undone. Certainly, Latimer was not only released and, early in October 1376, pardoned, but was then allowed to rejoin the Council. This was mainly under pressure from John of Gaunt, who, in his father's state of bad health and during his elder brother's terminal illness, had virtually taken over control of the government. Lancaster, indeed, had gone further. He attacked those who had been prominent in urging Latimer's disgrace: not only Sir Peter de la Mare, the late Speaker, who was imprisoned at Nottingham, but also William of Wykeham, bishop of Winchester, who had taken the Commons' side in the 'Good Parliament'. Wykeham, impeached in a great council convened in mid-October (shortly after Latimer had been pardoned), was denounced mainly on his record as keeper of the privy seal (1363–7) and chancellor (1367–71), the charges including misapplication of the revenues, taking bribes for the release of prisoners-of-war who were members of the French royal family, and (as in the case of Latimer and Neville) making illegal profits by buying up crown debts on the cheap;[4] and, after his conviction, Wykeham was deprived in November of the temporalities of his see. Lancaster was also able to manage the next parliament, the 'Bad Parliament' of January 1377, which not only confirmed Latimer's rehabilitation, but also accepted a petition now put forward by the Commons themselves, asking for his condemnation in the 'Good Parliament' to be reversed as having been brought about 'sanz due proces'.[5] What precisely was meant by this expression is not disclosed, but doubt may well have attached to the legal propriety of the Commons' recent adoption of the rôle of prosecutors. And although impeachments were occasionally to figure on the agenda of parliament in the course of the ten years which followed the 'Good Parliament', the prosecution was then always at the suit of the Crown, and undertaken by a royal minister: in one instance (1377) by the steward of the Household (Richard, lord Scrope) and, in the case of the politically more important impeachment of Bishop Despenser of Norwich for the failure of his Flemish crusade (1383), by the chancellor (Michael de la Pole).[6] Not until 1386, and then at the latter's expense, were such proceedings again both initiated and followed up by the Commons. The political agitation of the interim period arose mainly, however, over the constitution of the king's administration, a question which became additionally awkward during Richard II's minority, and over the financing and conduct of the war with France and her allies, a question no less troublesome. Developments came to a head in the parliaments of the time, and the very frequency with which parliament met—fifteen times in the decade, twice a year as often as not—attests the degree of governmental difficulty.

Politically embarrassing as had been Edward III's failure to retain a proper grip on the conduct of affairs during his last years, inherently more disturbing, once the old king had died and been succeeded by Richard II, was the fact of the latter's youth. (Richard was only ten years old when he came to the throne.) It was not so much that, if Richard died young and childless, his death would almost certainly give rise to violent debate as to who should succeed him, for that was a contingency which, although not unimaginable, remained only a possibility. (Although Richard's marriage, to Anne of Bohemia in 1382, must at first have given a promise of eventual relief on this score, the couple's failure to produce an heir meant not only, of course, that the problem remained, but that, as time passed, it would become one of even greater political significance and concern.) Rather, the mere fact of Richard's youth was disturbing, simply because effective government under a system of personal monarchy depended so much upon the king's own capacity that a royal minority was of itself bound to create discomfort and make for difficulty. Given such a situation, either a formal regency, based on close kinship, or conciliar control was essential. But if the latter plan was adopted, who would exercise that control? How would the councillors be chosen: by whom, in what circumstances (whether with parliamentary approval and as answerable to parliament, or not), and on the basis of what qualifications (whether according to rank and previous experience, or not)? Along what lines would the councillors operate? How independent would they be of the senior members of the royal family, Richard's uncles, and how free from parliamentary interference? And, indeed, for how long would conciliar control obtain? Moreover, to the uncertainty at Richard's accession as to the manner in which, especially in view of the ambitions of his uncles and parliament's opportunities for complaint, officials and other councillors might exercise the responsibility peculiarly attaching to a minority administration, would soon be added doubts as to the future development of the character and personality of the king himself. After all, he was bound to be subjected to a variety of influences, not least those emanating from existing associations (notably with former members of his father the Black Prince's household, his mother, and her other children, the Hollands) and from new companionships; and none of these, whether associations or companionships, could fail to have consequences of political significance.[7] When, and by whose encouragement, would he seek to break loose from constraints? There being no constitutional, or even customary, fixed limit to the duration of a royal minority, the problem as to when the king's theoretical responsibility might become direct and practical would become all the more acute when personal exercise of his prerogative rights could with decency no longer be denied him. And the young king, nothing if not precocious, was soon to show a high conceit of himself and his royal status. But once he had decided, for example, to choose his officials and councillors for himself, would he prove capable of choosing wisely, of discriminating between those who were ambitious to serve but generally regarded as unsuitable and those who were well qualified and also highly esteemed? Would he appoint those who could be relied upon to behave impartially and not just as friends and partisans, men who would tell him what he should know and ought to do, and not men who would tell him only what he wanted to hear and then let him do as he pleased? Would those whom he appointed conduct themselves honourably, and not exploit his inexperience and misuse their office and position for private advantage? Would he be able to withstand the importunities and blandishments of any such self-seekers as well as of his 'favourites'? And, supposing some of the magnates, the king's self-styled 'natural counsellors', criticised or openly opposed royal policy and the king's own actions, doing so most likely in parliament, where they could combine with least appearance of impropriety and also, conceivably, attract support from the Commons, would Richard resist this criticism or opposition? Would he construe indignant attacks on his ministers and friends, whether or not made in parliament, as in effect levelled against himself, and react accordingly? Here was a multiplicity of problems, none clear-cut and separate, but all predictable.

Edward III's death seemingly brought an easing of political tension and ill-humour. This was not to last, but it allowed Richard II's reign at least to begin in a more cordial atmosphere.[8] Even three days before Edward's death on 21 June 1377, William of Wykeham had been pardoned. And with only about a week of the new reign gone, Sir Peter de la Mare, the Commons' Speaker in the 'Good Parliament', was released from imprisonment at Nottingham and allowed to return to London.[9] John of Gaunt, hereditary high steward of England, was soon busy arranging for Richard's coronation on 16 July, and this event (which passed off well) was immediately followed by the appointment of a Council with executive powers. Appointed for the first time ever by letters patent, its members took the oath on 20 July in the king's presence.[10] This Council was composed of the chancellor and treasurer and twelve others, mostly magnates but in part representative too of the different political interests most powerful at the time. Lancaster was not himself a member, but his interests were indirectly consulted by the inclusion of his personal chancellor (Bishop Erghum of Salisbury) and Lord Latimer. Another sectional interest informally represented was that of the former household of the Black Prince, which since the latter's death had become Richard's own and, more recently, largely incorporated into the royal Household proper. Here, too, in positions of authority, were already installed other members of that princely household, notably Sir Hugh de Segrave, steward of the Black Prince's lands at the time of his death and now steward of the king's Household, and Sir Simon de Burley, formerly chief chamberlain to the Black Prince and now Richard's vice-chamberlain.[11] As such, Burley controlled the staff and operations of the King's Chamber, and was soon to make that place the 'power house' of the curialist party. However, so far as the Council was concerned, no sooner did Richard's first parliament meet (in October 1377) than the Commons, reverting to their attitude in the 'Good Parliament' under the leadership of Peter de la Mare, who was again their Speaker, demanded that anyone who had been reproved for his conduct as a councillor of the late king should be dismissed; and so Lord Latimer was turned out. Another five were also excluded, and only three new members were added to the remaining six of the original twelve. None of the king's uncles—John of Gaunt, Edmund of Langley and Thomas of Woodstock—joined this Council, but it was again made up of magnates. Of the nine appointed, only four, it was decided, would need to reside with the king continuously, although important matters were to be agreed by all. The councillors were to be paid stipends for their services, but none was to remain in office for more than a year or then be eligible for the next two.[12] The terms of appointment requested by the Commons were, in fact, similar to those they had demanded in 1376. Other of their common petitions even harked back to the Ordinances of 1311 (a sinister reference, even though it was expressly intended that what was proposed should only apply until the king was old enough to distinguish between right and wrong). What the Commons were requesting was that the king's chief officials, including the chancellor, the treasurer, the keeper of the privy seal, the chief justices, the chief baron of the Exchequer, the king's chamberlain, and the steward and the treasurer of his Household, should, like councillors, be nominated in parliament. The peers, with whom evidently the matter rested, acceded to the Commons' requests, but only in part: in view of the king's tender age, they replied, they would themselves elect the chancellor, the treasurer, the king's chamberlain, and the steward of the Household, but when parliament was not in session such appointments were to rest with the Council, as would also, and in any event, appointments to the other offices in question. [13] Another similar petition from the Commons, that those in charge of the king's person and his upbringing should also be nominated in parliament, was rejected by the Lords as a request 'trop chargeante et dure'. The Lords added, gratuitously, that they would consult with the officials of the Household in order to ensure that Household expenditure was moderate. [14]

When the second parliament of the reign met at Gloucester in October 1378, by which time, as previously agreed, the existing Council was due to be replaced, the Commons were quick to renew their pressure. At the very outset they requested to be informed of the names of such 'great officials', councillors, and governors of the king's person as were to act in the ensuing year;[15] and Richard, lord Scrope, the steward of the Household, replaced Bishop Houghton as chancellor before the session was a fortnight old. As regards other officials, no change was made. The Commons, moreover, were given to understand that, although such officials would continue to be appointed with the advice of the Lords, the appointment of councillors rested with the king, and that it would also be for him to decide whether their names should be communicated to the Commons. In fact, no councillors' names were either announced in parliament or recorded in the parliament-roll. However, *ex officio* members apart, a list of eight councillors was compiled soon after the Gloucester parliament ended and, to lay additional emphasis upon their obligation to attend assiduously, they were to be paid only daily wages, not an annual sum as their immediate predecessors had been. This new Council, too, lived out its term, remaining in office until the parliament of January 1380. All the same, and despite diligent service on the part of its members, it proved unable to work well or to act without support, and as early as February 1379 it needed to have recourse to a 'great council' of prelates and magnates[16] and in the following April to another parliament. Inadequacy of government finance (as will be seen later) was at the root of its troubles, but the very nature of its own constitution would seem to have made for added difficulty. Bishop Wykeham was a member, but otherwise the Council was 'strong in the courtier element, both the followers of the Black Prince with special retainers of the young king having their representatives' (Tout).[17] This evidently created suspicion, so much so that, as soon as opportunity offered, the Commons showed their dissatisfaction with the Council's conduct of affairs, not least with regard to its relations with the royal Household. In the parliament of April 1379 the Commons objected to the way in which, in order to raise crown loans, the Council had been making use of the services of Household knights and esquires who, carrying letters of privy seal with the tags left blank ('les cowes [queues] blankes'), had sought out likely lenders with whose names, and with the sums to be demanded of them, they had then completed the writs, threatening any who declined to pay such forced loans with summonses to appear before the Council.[18] The Commons went on, moreover, to petition for and obtain the appointment of a committee of lords to examine 'the estate of the king', including Household expenditure.[19] Admittedly, if this committee was to be given sufficient time to carry out its investigation, there was no body to which it could report save the Council, and this was what was required of it. But the very appointment of such a committee implied a warning to the Council as well as to the Household. So too did the appointment of one of the committee's members, John, lord Cobham, to replace Sir Simon de Burley, the under-chamberlain, as the young king's tutor or personal guardian.[20]

However, despite such correctives, the Council's handling of affairs evidently continued to be regarded as so unsatisfactory that when parliament again met, in January 1380, a fresh mode of government was proposed. For the Commons now not only asked for the discharge of the existing Council, but also demanded that the type of Council so far employed (an elective council of magnates serving for a limited period) should be discarded in favour of a Council composed simply of the king's five 'principal officers', viz. the chancellor, the treasurer, the keeper of the privy seal, the 'chief' chamberlain, and the steward of the Household. The reason the Commons gave was that the king was now 'de bone discretion et de belle stature' and roughly as old as Edward III had been when crowned, at which time, so they said, those same officials had been the king's only councillors. This had not, in fact, been the case in 1327; but the Commons, naturally untroubled by their own ignorance, then proceeded to demand that the five officials in question should be 'elected' in the parliament, that they themselves should be told who they were, and that the ministers, once appointed, should remain in office until the next parliament.[21] What the Commons must have been mainly anxious to achieve was a greater measure of ministerial responsibility to parliament, for of all the five officials to whom reference was made, only one was, in fact, replaced. That one, however, was the chancellor, Richard, lord Scrope, who on 30 January (when the parliament was a fortnight old) made room for Archbishop Sudbury. Obviously still not altogether contented with their request as it stood, the Commons went on to demand the appointment of a commission of enquiry into the running of the central administration, a commission similar, in general purpose, to the one appointed in the previous parliament, which had not, presumably, made any report. Again there was to be an investigation of the state of the royal Household, but the commission's enquiry into all the royal finances was now to reach back to the beginning of the reign; and the commission itself was differently constituted, comprising not only, as before, ten peers (of whom six, including Lord Latimer, had been members of the previous commission), but also, by a novel mode of enlargement, five representatives of the Commons as well, including their Speaker.[22] When, although this session closed in March with a request that parliament should not, in order to grant taxation, be reconvened before Michaelmas 1381,[23] another parliament did meet for that very purpose at Northampton later in the year (November 1380), the Commons were now rather apathetic both as regards the commission of enquiry and the constitution of the government. Although the commission had failed to act, the Commons evidently still believed it had a rôle to play, for they now requested that its members, already given authority by letters sealed in the last parliament, should be charged to begin their 'serche' on 20 January 1381, and also that suitable wages should be paid them for these future services.[24] As regards the Council, for how long after the last parliament it had remained restricted, if indeed at all, to the king's 'principal officers', cannot be said. But if, as the Commons had desired in the January 1380 parliament, that restriction had applied, clearly by the time of the Northampton parliament of November following it did so no longer. For when the Commons then asked that none of the five should be removed before the next parliament, the answer was that the king would do as seemed him best 'by the advice of his Council',[25] a council which, in the context, could only mean one which included others than the officials themselves. Evidently, the Commons had been satisfied with the ministry as it stood. But the answer to their request both safeguarded the royal prerogative from a repetition of recent attempts to undermine it in favour of parliamentary intervention and, if not so clearly, at least implied the possibility of change. And some changes were, in fact, soon made: before the end of January 1381 Sir William Beauchamp (formerly a member of the Black Prince's council) had been succeeded as acting chief chamberlain by Sir Aubrey de Vere, uncle of Robert de Vere, earl of Oxford and hereditary chamberlain; and on 1 February Bishop Brantingham of Exeter was replaced as treasurer by Sir Robert Hales, prior of the hospital of St John, one of the lay peers.[26] No further change took place until rendered unavoidable by the Peasants' Revolt, during which the chancellor (Sudbury) and the treasurer (Hales) were murdered, both of them in London on 13 June.

After these and other horrific events, it was nearly two months before a normally constituted government was properly restored. No treasurer was to succeed Hales until 10 August. And, although some steps were taken to make it appear that a government of sorts was still in being, appointments to even the chancellorship were only interim measures. The earl of

Arundel's appointment on 14 June (the morrow of Sudbury's death) was simply to make possible the issue of those pardons and manumissions which the king had promised the Essex peasants at Mile End, and was expressly just for that one day. The appointment two days later (the morrow of Wat Tyler's death) of Sir Hugh Segrave, the steward of the Household, was also intended to be no more than temporary, and Segrave did not even relinquish his Household office until, on 10 August, he also ceased to be chancellor, then becoming treasurer of the Exchequer instead. This change of rôle on Segrave's part and the appointment of his successor in the chancellorship, Archbishop Courtenay (Sudbury's successor in the primacy), both took place on the first day of a great council of prelates and magnates which, meeting at Reading, made the 'election' of the two chief officers of state its prime business. But whereas the new treasurer, Segrave, was destined to remain in office until January 1386 (and, incidentally, his immediate successor as steward of the Household, Sir John Montague, for a year longer still), Courtenay resigned the great seal in under four months (on 30 November), being succeeded four days later by Richard, lord Scrope, who had been chancellor previously (the second chancellor of the reign).

It was before the end of the first of the two sessions of the parliament which had met on 3 November 1381 that Courtenay went out of office. His dismissal may have as much reflected John of Gaunt's recovery of political influence in this aftermath of the Peasants' Revolt (for Lancaster was no friend of Courtenay's) as did the choice of his successor (for Scrope had long been Lancaster's friend), but it appears that the Commons, too, had little faith in Courtenay as the king's chief minister. Certainly when, after intercommuning with the Lords, the Commons demanded the appointment of yet another set of commissioners of enquiry with a view to a reform of the royal administration in greater detail than had been proposed in either 1379 or 1380, they also asked that, once an ordinance had been made touching the king's person and his Household, 'a wise, discreet, and the most competent person to be found in the kingdom, either spiritual or temporal', should be appointed as chancellor, to help the commissioners, now headed by Lancaster, to reform the Chancery. (It was said that the clerks of Chancery needed weeding out, having become for the most part too ostentatiously prosperous, 'grown too bulky in body and purse, and too much given to wearing fur'.)[27] That request must have preceded Courtenay's resignation, and had possibly helped bring it about. Moreover, although the Commons went on to request that the new appointment should be made 'by the advice of the king', this can only mean that, while they were agreeable to the king's being consulted in the matter, the choice should rest with parliament, or at least that parliament's approval was essential. Presumably, Scrope's appointment enjoyed that approval. Whether or not this appointment pleased the king to begin with, it did not (as will be seen) continue to do so for very long. And pleasing the king was recognisably becoming a factor of growing importance. The Commons of the parliament of November 1381 were already well aware of this.

Richard was still only fourteen years old, but in view of the prominent and heady part he had played in the crisis of the Peasants' Revolt, the fact that his marriage was now immediately impending, and his evident desire to impose his personal will on the conduct of affairs, the Commons had every reason to be worried about his rôle, and about those who were influencing its development. The parliament of November 1381, in fact, had hardly begun before the Commons, anxious for reform, were referring to 'defautes . . . entour la persone le Roi';[28] and they then went on to request that bad officials and councillors should be turned out, and that the most competent and prudent lords and 'bachelors' available should be chosen to attend upon the king and to form his Council.[29] The Lords were clearly of the same mind, and when, as they advised, the king allowed the commission of enquiry into 'l'Estat et Governaill de la Persone nostre dit Seigneur' as well as into the state of the Household, they added that it would be proper for general reform of government to begin at the 'Principal membre, q'est le Roi mesmes'.[30] Evidently, with the Commons wishing to be informed of the new appointments (as well as of the content of the expected ordinance), changes other than that of the chancellor were anticipated. The only person actually mentioned in the parliament-roll as unsatisfactory was the king's confessor (Thomas Rushook) who, although the Commons had requested his expulsion from office, was not dismissed, but merely charged (in the presence of the king and Lords) to stay away from the court, except at the four principal church festivals of the year.[31] But the custody of the great seal apart, another ministry was to be affected, for on the day of parliament's adjournment (13 December) John Fordham was superseded by William Dighton as keeper of the privy seal.

Such evidence as survives does not indicate that Fordham was dismissed. Perhaps he simply resigned. After all, he had been keeper of the privy seal ever since Richard II's accession and, especially in view of his recent provision to the bishopric of Durham and the imminence of his consecration, he may himself have welcomed the move. However, even if he did resign, it still may well have been under parliamentary pressure. He was notoriously unpopular (witness the demand for his head, made during the Peasants' Revolt by the men of Kent, who had later gone on to plunder the wine cellar in his house in the Strand),[32] and this unpopularity was possibly held against him in this first parliament after the revolt. But perhaps not only that: with his once having been secretary and executor to the Black Prince, general receiver and keeper of the privy seal in the short-lived household of Richard as prince of Wales, and now, having held his present office since the beginning of the reign, so long resident at court, it was possibly thought that he was too liable to become dangerously amenable to the king's will. (The keepership of the privy seal was the only important governmental office not to have changed hands since Richard's accession.) If parliament was in fact moved to urge Fordham's dismissal, no doubt his elevation to the episcopate made it easier for him to "bow out" with composure. However this may be, the appointment of his successor, Dighton, the senior clerk in the privy seal office, was possibly regarded as only a stop-gap measure. Dighton did, nevertheless, retain office until August 1382, when Walter Skirlaw, a Chancery clerk mostly employed in diplomacy, entered upon a long tenure of the keepership of the privy seal which only ended when did Michael de la Pole's chancellorship, in October 1386.

The day of Dighton's promotion, the last day of the first session of the 1381 parliament, also witnessed what must have seemed at the time another useful step. For it was then reported to the Commons that the earl of Arundel and Sir Michael de la Pole had been 'elected', appointed and sworn to attend upon the king's person in his Household, there to counsel and 'govern' him.[33] Considering the different origins, personalities and attitudes of the two peers, not to mention the king's probably adverse reaction to such surveillance, it is extremely doubtful whether this measure ever stood any real chance of success. Certainly, the circumstances in which, as early as July 1382, Lord Scrope was dismissed from the chancellorship, hardly suggest that the intention or conditions of the appointment of the king's 'governors' were being fulfilled. For it was Richard's independently exercised liberality towards favoured courtiers, which, as expressed in unjustifiable and excessive grants, particularly of escheated lands, Scrope refused to countenance, that led to the latter's dismissal. (He is said to have then told the king that never again would he serve him as an official.)[34] That this event created a great stir is confirmed by the fact that it was only after a hiatus of two months that, on 9 September, a successor was appointed, namely, Robert Braybrook, bishop of London. A kinsman of the king (on Richard's mother's side) and the keeper of his signet during the first four years of the reign, Braybrook was hardly the man to exercise much restraint over the king, or to reverse the growing inclination on the part of courtiers to establish themselves in a stronger position. In fact, Braybrook's appointment was, in a way, symptomatic of developments that were soon to intensify Household control.

The problem raised by the royal Household was perhaps

most obviously a financial one, and when the parliamentary commissions of enquiry of 1379, 1380 and 1381 had been told to look into the 'estate of the Household', it was Household expenditure that was chiefly in question. But developments were taking place in the Household and affecting members of its staff which, although control of the Household's operations and activities was always difficult enough, could only make it more difficult still. Even as a general rule, there was a tendency for Household officials to assume external administrative and judicial functions, and so for the Household itself, as a multi-departmental institution, to become more effectively influential in the work of government proper. The royal administration had originated in the *curia regis*, and it was always liable, in this way and that, to 'revert to type'. In any case, with its own secretariat and accounting offices paralleling those great offices of state which had long since 'gone out of court', it was all but impossible to maintain any strict lines of demarcation; and the court was always ready to encourage developments which would help keep control of the running of things 'within the family'. Of course, all this was inevitable under a system of personal monarchy, where naturally the king was inclined to rely upon those who, as members of his Household, were constantly close at hand, at his immediate beck and call, and who themselves, having the ear of the king, stood to benefit from this propinquity. An early recognisable pointer to this state of affairs was the transfer or interchange of official personnel as between the Household and the more formal departments of government like the Chancery and the Exchequer. In this connexion no importance need be attached to the fact that Lord Scrope, twice chancellor in Richard's first five years, had been steward of the Household in the meantime, because this appointment took place when the king had little if any personal influence on the conduct of affairs. But it was no doubt different with Scrope's immediate successor as steward, Sir Hugh Segrave, who after two years became treasurer of the Exchequer, for not only did he merit the king's trust as a valued retainer and official of his late father, but was to remain at the

Exchequer for the next four and a half years (until January 1386), that is, almost throughout the period of growth of the curialist party, and by when it was possible for him to be succeeded as treasurer by John Fordham, the former keeper of the privy seal. Of course, the number of men able and willing to serve in such offices was limited. But employment in high Household office, whether before or after service in a major department of state, would seem, by and large, to have generated much greater sympathy for royal government by prerogative than for royal government under parliamentary control. More likely still to promote prerogative government *via* the Household was the tendency for a doubling-up of rôles and functions to take place, and this development was already under way by 1381. In January that year William Packington, who had been treasurer of the Household since the earliest days of the reign, was appointed for life as chancellor of the Exchequer, albeit still retaining his Household office.[35] It might appear at first sight as if a reverse tendency is to be discerned in the appointment, in May 1381, of John Bacon, one of the two chamberlains of the Exchequer, as keeper of the king's signet and, in November 1382, as receiver of the King's Chamber also, all three of which posts Bacon continued to hold concurrently for a time; but Bacon was another who had served Richard before his accession, and was regarded by him as a personal friend (witness the part the king played in arranging Bacon's funeral service in Westminster Abbey in 1385 and his personal attendance at the exequial mass).[36] It needs only to be added that Bacon's custody of the signet was to begin its greatly extended use, a development positively encouraged by Michael de la Pole when chancellor.

Bishop Braybrook, appointed chancellor in September 1382, held office for only six months, during which time there met two unusually short (although busy) parliaments. It was on the day when the second was dissolved (10 March 1383) that Braybrook resigned, and it can hardly be doubted that he did so because of parliamentary dissatisfaction. Certainly, the Commons had petitioned for changes among the 'highest' offices of state, asking that the king, acting with the advice of the great lords, and impartially, would choose those most loyal and capable, that parliament should be told who they were, and that they should not be removed without reasonable cause. The king agreed, saying that he would make no further changes before the next parliament.[37] The chancellorship, however, was the only high office then to change hands. Moreover, a successor to Braybrook was not named in parliament. It was not, in fact, until three days after parliament's dissolution, 13 March 1383, that Sir Michael de la Pole was appointed chancellor (the great seal having been only temporarily entrusted to John Waltham, the keeper of the rolls of the Chancery). Had the decision to appoint Michael been taken before the session ended, it is doubtful whether it would have pleased the Commons. For whereas, in this last parliament (as in its two predecessors), they themselves had opposed John of Gaunt's plan for attacking France indirectly by means of an expedition to Spain, and had preferred the alternative scheme of a Flemish 'crusade', with the result that Lancaster had left the parliament in disgust, Michael was an old adherent of Lancaster's. The new chancellor was soon to show himself in favour of Lancaster's ideas and ill-disposed to his opponents, and it is quite possible that Michael's appointment was partly intended to mollify the duke. However this may be, it looks as if the appointment was deliberately put off until parliament had gone down, perhaps out of fear of repercussions in the Lower House, perhaps also, by avoiding parliament's involvement in the nomination, in order to emphasise the prerogatival nature of the appointment. It was in such circumstances that Michael came to take charge of the great seal, a custody he was to retain for over three and a half years, the longest of the reign thus far.

It was only natural that, with the mere passage of time, the king would intensify his efforts to break loose from leading-strings and assume a decisive personal rôle in the conduct of affairs. But what mainly aroused opposition to this among the great nobles and in parliament were the means which Richard employed and the ends which he appeared to have in mind and was aiming at. These, means and ends, were too confused for general comfort. In aid of prerogative government, he enhanced the political and administrative functions of the Household, especially those of his Chamber and the Signet Office. But then so much of the effort of this system seemed to go into controlling royal patronage, which meant in effect providing the courtiers with offices and rewards, a process which proved so much to the benefit of 'favourites' and other personal friends, like Robert de Vere, Sir Simon de Burley, Sir John Beauchamp of Holt, and the king's secretaries, first John Bacon and then Richard Metford, not to mention the chancellor himself. The latter, far from merely tolerating the system, actively encouraged it by personal participation. In fact, following his appointment, Michael had soon identified himself with the court party, and from then on he persistently aided and abetted the development of the king's own personal power. Perhaps the most straightforwardly practical way in which he did so, certainly the most easily detectable (from the Chancery records themselves), was to accept warrants under the signet as entirely sufficient for issuance of letters under the great seal. And while Michael was chancellor, use of the signet became quite conventional, especially after the spring of 1385 when Metford became Richard's secretary: by the autumn of that year as many grants were being warranted by this most personal seal of the king 'as by all other authorities combined', and by the end of Michael's chancellorship the signet 'had become the most common means of moving the great seal' (A. Tuck).[38]

Dependent as this practice was on Michael's co-operation as chancellor, directly behind and inciting its development was, of course, Richard himself, and he was already quite enamoured of ideas of prerogatival authority. When, for example, in the parliament of October 1383, the first to meet after Michael's appointment, a bill was presented on behalf of Sir Robert Pleasington, the chief baron of the Exchequer, asking that a charter of general pardon, previously allowed him, should be renewed with the assent of parliament, and Richard, 'par sa bouche propre', granted the petition, he went out of his way to insist that no such charter as obviously touched his prerogative ('sa propre Grace et Regalie') should be confirmed in parliament or authorised by anybody but himself, and that nothing else should be done privily or publicly in derogation of his 'droite Regalie et Dignitee'.[39] Since he was capable of such a pronouncement at the age of sixteen, it is hardly surprising that when, two years later (in 1385), the Commons requested to be told who were to be 'les principalx officers' and other members of the Council, so implying dissatisfaction with the existing constitution of the government, and the king refused to entertain the idea of any change, he did so in terms clearly expressing his conviction that such appointments were matters strictly within his own personal discretion: 'il y ad officers sufficeantz au present, et le Roi les changera quant lui plerra'.[40] It was this principle and its dependencies that were mainly at stake in the parliament of 1386. The impeachment of Michael de la Pole may not unreasonably be construed as, in effect, an attack upon the whole scheme for government by personal prerogative.

In how implacably hostile a manner parliament behaved towards the régime in 1386 may be inferred from the threat of deposition to which the king was subjected by the leaders of the opposition in the Lords, as well as from the attack upon his chief minister undertaken by the Commons. But the Commons' attack was serious enough. Were there to be any doubt on this score, it would be resolved simply by reference to the renewal of the procedure of impeachment by the Commons, a mode of prosecution to which *they* had had recourse only once before (in 1376). The Commons, by their criticism and demands for reform in parliament after parliament since then, had been actively asserting themselves; but what they were party to in 1386 was of a different order of opposition. And if any further proof were needed, it would be furnished not only by the king's immediate resistance, but especially by the violence of his reaction as it was to appear in 1387.

Notes

1 Robert Stratford, bishop of Chichester, chancellor, and Roger Northburgh, bishop of Coventry and Lichfield, treasurer, both dismissed on 1 December 1340. The former was replaced by Sir Robert Bourchier on 14 December following, the latter by Sir Robert Parving (formerly chief justice of the King's Bench) on 15 January 1341. Parving succeeded Bourchier as chancellor on 28 October 1341 and, when he died on 26 August 1343, was followed by Sir Robert Saddington (chief baron of the Exchequer), who remained chancellor until 26 October 1345. The great seal thereafter until 1371 was in the custody of ecclesiastics, all of whom from 1349 were bishops. So, from 1345, were all the treasurers of that period (save, at the time of their appointment, William Edington and Simon Langham, but then they soon, whilst still in office, became bishops).

2 *Rot. Parl.* II, 323–5. For a detailed and eminently fair discussion of these charges and their background, reference should be made to G. A. Holmes, *The Good Parliament* (Oxford, 1975), 65–90. May McKisack, in *The Oxford History of England: the Fourteenth Century, 1307–1399* (Oxford, 1959), 391, thought that Lyons's denial of the charge about the loan of 20,000 marks was possibly correct, and was of the opinion that 'the guilt of the accused may have been assumed rather too easily by later historians'.

3 If this charge is to be believed, the government was, in effect, having to pay 10,000 marks for the 5,000 marks which was all that was required to make up the difference between the loan that was offered free of interest and the loan on which interest was charged. Evidently, the interest-free loan was not taken up.

4 *The Anonimalle Chronicle, 1333 to 1381*, ed. V. H. Galbraith (Manchester, 1927), 99–100.

5 *Rot. Parl.*, II, 372.

6 Ibid., III, 10–12, 153. For a full discussion of this question of responsibility for prosecutions in late fourteenth century impeachments, see *Transactions of the Royal Historical Society*, 4th ser., XXIV (1942), T. F. T. Plucknett, 'The Origin of Impeachment'; 5th ser., II (1952), 'State Trials under Richard II'.

7 In this connexion we need only recall the Poitevins and Savoyards of Henry III's reign, and the friendship of Edward II and Piers Gaveston.

8 *Chronicon Angliae 1328–1388* (R.S.), ed. E. Maunde Thompson, 146–51.

9 For the circumstances of Sir Peter's release and return to London, see *Nottingham Medieval Studies*, II (1958), 32–3.

10 *Rot. Parl.*, III, 386; *CPR, 1377–81*, 19; and see *E.H.R.*, XLI, 246–51, N. B. Lewis, 'The Continual Council in the early years of Richard II, 1377–1380'.

11 Tout, *Chapters*, III, 329–32.

12 *Rot. Parl*, III, 6, 16; Tout, *Chapters*, III, 333–4.

13 *Rot. Parl.*, III, 16; for the significance of this petition, see *B.I.H.R.*, XXVI (1953), 200–13, J. G. Edwards, 'Some Common Petitions in Richard II's first Parliament'.

14 *Rot. Parl.*, III, 7.

15 Ibid., 35–6.

16 Tout, *Chapters*, III, 346–7.

17 Ibid., 343.

18 *Rot. Parl.*, III, 62.

19 Ibid., 57.

20 Tout, *Chapters*, III, 349.

21 *Rot. Parl.*, III, 73.

22 Ibid.

23 Ibid., 75.

24 Ibid., 93.

25 Ibid., 96.

26 Tout, *Chapters*, III, 356.

27 *Rot. Parl.*, III, 101, ¶20.

28 Ibid., 100, ¶17.

29 Ibid., 101, ¶17.

30 Ibid., ¶18.

31 Ibid.

32 *Anonimalle Chronicle*, 139, 141.

33 *Rot. Parl.*, III, 104.

34 *Chronicon Angliae 1328–1388*, 354.

35 Tout, *Chapters*, III, 357.

36 Ibid., 358; IV, 334; V, 215.

37 *Rot. Parl.*, III, 147.

38 Anthony Tuck, *Richard II and the English Nobility* (London, 1973), 67.

39 *Rot. Parl.*, III, 165.

40 Ibid., 213, ¶38.

III

Diplomatic and military difficulties

So far as England was concerned, the renewal of the French war late in 1369 was diplomatically ill-prepared for. Edward III's earlier system of alliances in the Low Countries and with the Empire had long since broken down, so that when he renewed the war it was virtually on the basis of his own resources alone. Charles V of France and his brother Philip, duke of Burgundy (who on Charles's death in 1380 was to assume immediate control of the government of France on behalf of his young nephew, Charles VI), had the support of allies who, because of close dependence upon France in time of need, were now to give more effective help than the English had ever had from theirs, even in the heyday of the Edwardian achievement. In 1369 France already had firm allies in Scotland[1] and Castile.[2] The Scottish alliance was renewed in 1370. In Castile, Henry of Trastamara's usurpation was too recent for him to dispense with the French support which had won him the crown of his half-brother, Peter the Cruel, and to retain that support he must needs be prepared to intervene actively in the Anglo-French conflict. The marriages of Edward III's sons, John of Gaunt and Edmund of Langley, successively (in 1371 and 1372), to Peter's surviving daughters—the former to the elder daughter (Constance) who, as her father's heir-designate, represented the Castilian legitimist cause—emphasised a threat to the Trastamaran dynasty which only confirmed Henry's reliance upon France and consequently his readiness to assist her. In comparison, the Anglo-Portuguese alliance of 1373 was of non-effect, at least for the time being. Nor, at this juncture, did much meaning attach to the English alliance with Navarre. So far as Brittany was concerned—and the succession to the duchy was still disputed—no firm trust could be put in Duke John IV by either party.[3] Louis de Mâle, count of Flanders, was virtually neutral, but then, given the marriage, early in 1369, of his daughter and heir (Margaret) to Philip of Burgundy, he was likely to become more than less friendly towards France, especially if there should again be trouble with the great Flemish communes and, in any case, when, as he aged, his son-in-law's succession to the county became a more sharply defined prospect.[4]

Once the Anglo-French war had re-started, inevitably the diplomacy of the parties became also conditional upon the progress of hostilities. And, on the whole, these went much better for the French than the English. In 1372 French arms had not only retaken all Poitou and Saintonge, but had restricted English-held territory in Guienne to Bordeaux, its neighbourhood, and the Gascon coastal strip farther south (including Bayonne). This was the year, too, in which a large English convoy proceeding to the relief of those parts under the earl of Pembroke had been destroyed off La Rochelle by Castilian galleys. Admittedly, a succession of English armies of not inconsiderable strength had already invaded France, ravaging whole areas in different regions. But even the most ambitious of such *chevauchées*, that led by John of Gaunt from Calais through central France to Bordeaux in 1373, was no more productive of any positively useful result than earlier expeditions. However, the French had certainly not been so successful as to destroy English hopes of recovery. It was not long, in fact, before they themselves were ready for a respite; and although negotiations for a peace settlement, entered into at Bruges in 1375, and seriously pursued, broke down over the chronic problem of the tenurial status of Aquitaine, a truce was then agreed (thanks to papal mediation), and that truce was later extended to 24 June 1377.

The expiry of this truce almost precisely coincided with Edward III's death, and it was the French who, taking advantage of the distractions attendant upon that event in England, now took the initiative. Louis of Anjou moved on Bordeaux, and Philip of Burgundy on Calais. Neither was to succeed in his intention, but that very summer the English south coast was subjected to the shock of direct attack by a combined naval force of French and Castilians, in the course of which considerable damage was done at Hastings, Rotting-dean, Portsmouth, Dartmouth and Plymouth; the Isle of Wight was temporarily occupied; and Rye and Poole were burnt. Fortunately, from the English point of view, Charles V's formal annexation of Brittany to the French crown in 1378 proved a costly mistake, for not only did it provoke successful rebellion in the duchy, but once again allowed the English an opportunity to pose as the protectors of Breton independence and to obtain from Duke John IV the right to garrison Brest. Cherbourg was also now acquired, by lease from Charles of Navarre. However, attempts in the same year to insert fresh links in the chain of bridgeheads along the north coast of France, at Harfleur by the earl of Arundel and at Saint-Malo (a five months' siege) by John of Gaunt, had turned out badly. Then, in 1379, an expeditionary force, on passage to Brittany, was mostly shipwrecked off Ireland. In 1380 a large army under Thomas of Woodstock's command marched from Calais, via Champagne, to Brittany, only to find on arrival that, following the death of Charles V in September, Duke John IV was already negotiating with Charles VI's councillors a return to his French allegiance, leaving Woodstock with no alternative but to return home in the following spring, shortly after the conclusion of the new Franco-Breton treaty of April 1381. So had been added to the sorry tale another costly and, in terms of strategical effect, futile enterprise: under the circumstances, possibly one that did more harm than good. Nothing ever seemed to go right. But there was always something which seemed to open up a fresh prospect and induce optimism. The papal schism of 1378 was just such an occurrence: it immediately looked as if it might have a galvanising effect on English diplomacy.[5] It certainly added a new aspect.

When all the French-born cardinals who, at Rome in April 1378, had been party to the election of Urban VI shortly afterwards repudiated him and, at Fondi in September following, elected Clement VII instead, they not only counted upon a return to Avignon, but also assumed that Charles V of France, who had so far supported their cause, would continue to do so, and that his allies would adopt his policy. If in some instances only after a delay, these assumptions proved correct. Meanwhile, England had promptly adhered to Urban. Backed by the German Diet, so had the Emperor, Charles IV, the head of the house of Luxembourg and hereditary king of Bohemia; and when Charles died (November 1378) his son and successor, Wenzel IV, maintained his policy. It was now obviously to Urban's interest to promote a league or coalition between the countries which supported him against those which favoured the Avignonese anti-pope, and in the second year of the schism the Roman pope took steps to create an alliance between England and the Empire, cemented by a marriage between Richard II and Anne, Wenzel's sister. It was not, however, until May 1381 that this Anglo-German alliance was concluded, and though the marriage took place (in January 1382), it was clear by 1383 that the alliance itself was not a success. Admittedly, it had helped maintain Urban's obedience intact. But it had failed to extend it. Indeed, whereas England had hoped for help against France as schismatic, Wenzel had shown his preference for the rôle of mediator between the two, a rôle which so little suited either England or the Roman Curia as to strengthen at least *their* common interest. For the main concerns of both still coincided. Urban had always needed to distract the French from military intervention in Italy on Clement's behalf, and to this end to prolong and, if possible, exacerbate English hostility towards France; and England was still prepared to continue the war, if no longer by invasion of France proper, then indirectly by attacks on her schismatical allies. Urban evidently soon resigned himself to this change of the English plan, for it was in fact in aid of expeditions against allies of France—expeditions that took English armies into

Flanders and Spain as well as into Scotland—that the Roman pope issued his bulls of crusade. The air of religiosity the bulls lent to those enterprises was no doubt specious, but they were of probably quite considerable financial benefit. This was at least the case with Bishop Despenser of Norwich's Flemish 'crusade' of 1383. Here again it was a previously unforeseen event which provided the English with a fresh opportunity.

Although it was in 1379 that, led by Ghent, the Flemish communes revolted against their count, Louis de Mâle, it was not until January 1382 that the English parliament first discussed the question of lending them military assistance. And even when parliament did so, it was divided over it: what the Lords commended was John of Gaunt's wish to lead an expedition to Portugal, there to join his brother Edmund's forces with a view to enforcing his claim to the Castilian throne; it was the Commons who, objecting to supporting by taxation what they chose to regard as the duke's private ambitions in Spain, preferred an expedition into Flanders. However, not until January 1383 did parliament finally decide to adopt the 'voie de Flandres' as opposed to the 'voie d'Espaigne', entrusting the leadership of the Flemish expedition to Bishop Despenser of Norwich when the latter undertook to conduct it as an Urbanist crusade supported by papal bulls. What had directly prompted the decision to intervene, in fact, was the great victory of a large French army at Roosebeke in November 1382 which, nevertheless, was so catastrophic a defeat for the Flemish rebels as to render English prospects of success extremely doubtful from the start. Indeed, Despenser's expedition, which lasted from May to October 1383, was a complete fiasco, militarily and otherwise, so much so that the bishop was impeached, for his misjudgments and errors of one kind and another, in the parliament that followed his inglorious return. And it was the chancellor, De la Pole, who conducted the prosecution. Never thereafter did the rebel cause in Flanders recover its earlier momentum. And whatever hopes of its doing so remained, and of the possibility of any English success in Flanders, they were virtually doomed to frustration when, on the death of Louis de Mâle early in 1384, Philip of Burgundy possessed himself of the county (in right of his wife), and in April 1385 effectively ensured his permanent security in the territory by the great diplomatic *coup* represented by the marriage of both his son and heir and a daughter into the dynasty of the Wittelsbachs (hereditary counts of Holland, Hainault, and Zeeland). Moreover, that the Flemish rebel cause, meaning by now the resistance of Ghent alone, could no longer expect any continuously satisfactory help from England was made clear in the summer of 1385. For then, despite the fact that it was from bases in Flanders that a large French army threatened a seaborne invasion of southern England, the English preferred to attack by invasion France's allies the Scots, rather than send help to the Gantois. When, by the treaty of Tournai (December 1385), Burgundy imposed his peace on the whole of Flanders, whatever embarrassment France had suffered from that quarter was at an end, and the way was clear for the preparation of the even greater threat of a French invasion of England in the summer of 1386. Admittedly, when parliament met in October 1385 a promise of modest assistance had been made to the Gantois. But even the promise of help came too late, let alone help itself. In any case, parliament now showed positive interest in John of Gaunt's ambition to make good his claim to the crown of Castile, appropriated substantial funds to that end, and so made possible the expedition he took out to the Iberian peninsula in the summer of 1386. No doubt the auspices for Lancaster's crusade in Spain were now more favourable than ever they had been for Despenser's in Flanders, for whereas Despenser's expedition had followed the French defeat of the Flemish rebels at Roosebeke, Lancaster's had been largely prompted and encouraged by the recent and overwhelming Portuguese defeat of the Castilians under the second king of the Trastamaran line, John I, at Aljubarrota (14 August 1385). The absence from England of the oldest member of the royal family and the most powerful of the nobility doubtless contributed to the scare caused by the threat of French invasion. Almost certainly the removal of John of

Gaunt's personal influence contributed even more to the political crisis precipitated by the military panic, the political crisis which brought about the overthrow of Richard II's first curialist party, including the fall of his chancellor, the earl of Suffolk.

Notes

1 For Anglo-Scottish relations in this period, see the chapter, by James Campbell, entitled 'England, Scotland and the Hundred Years War in the Fourteenth Century' in *Europe in the Late Middle Ages* (London, 1965), ed. J. R. Hale, J. R. L. Highfield and B. Smalley.

2 For Anglo- and Franco-Castilian and Anglo-Portuguese relations, P. E. Russell, *The English Intervention in Spain and Portugal in the time of Edward III and Richard II* (Oxford, 1955), is indispensable.

3 For Breton external affairs, see the chapter, by John Le Patourel, entitled 'The King and the Princes in fourteenth-century France' in *Europe in the Late Middle Ages*, cited in note 1, and the more detailed treatment supplied by M. Jones, *Ducal Brittany, 1364–1399: Relations with England and France during the Reign of Duke John IV* (Oxford, 1970).

4 See Richard Vaughan, *Philip the Bold* (London, 1962), Chapter Two.

5 See E. Perroy, *L'Angleterre et le Grande Schisme d'Occident* (Paris, 1933).

IV

The problem of finance

The resumption of the war with France in 1369 brought in its train a continuing fiscal crisis. If diplomacy was costly, military campaigns, not to mention the upkeep of coastal fortresses and bridgeheads in France, were even more so. On this score alone, parliamentary taxation was never enough to meet the government's demands. All the same, such grants, possibly felt to be justified after an absence of direct taxation between 1359 and 1371, became not only very heavy, but heavier than before.[1] Direct taxes, whether levied on parishes in 1371–2, or by tenths and fifteenths, or in the first poll tax of 1377, yielded in the last seven years of Edward III approximately £186,000. The first eight years of Richard II yielded something over twice that amount: Richard's first four years (1377–1381 inclusive), in taxes taking the form of tenths and fifteenths and, in 1379 and 1381, poll taxes, yielded approximately £196,000, and the next four (down to 1385 inclusive) approximately £190,000. All the grants of these last four years were in the form of tenths and fifteenths, the largest single grant, the one and a half tenths and fifteenths granted in 1385, being the last grant made by parliament before the crisis of 1386. It was again taxation in the form of tenths and fifteenths that Michael de la Pole demanded at the opening of the parliament of 1386. But what he now asked for was no less than four such subsidies (equivalent to some £150,000).[2] It was most likely this staggeringly high demand that precipitated the chancellor's impeachment.

Heavy though taxation had been since 1371, the government's unease at its inadequacy, an unease evidently shared by parliament, was for some time reflected in the changes of form of levy. Tenths and fifteenths were what people were used to, and the amounts granted in this form were at least predictable. But this system, with levies based on counties, hundreds and vills, and upon towns, the assessments of which had been fixed in amount ever since 1334, was for economic reasons inequitable, and in any case full of anomalies. Hence recourse to the one levy on parishes and, later, the short series of poll taxes. But these taxes, too, contained anomalies productive of difficulties of assessment, and the last of the poll taxes (1381), mainly because of its weight of incidence, provoked such a reaction and social upheaval in the Peasants' Revolt as made any repetition of taxation in that form quite unthinkable. On the whole, though, parliament was obviously willing to co-operate in a situation in which heavy governmental expenditure was inevitable; and, in this period, it was only in the 'Good Parliament' of 1376, the Gloucester parliament of 1378, and the first session of the parliament which followed the Peasants' Revolt, that parliament refused to respond to the government's demands for direct taxes. But parliament first needed to be convinced that the government had a case, and, of equal importance, it wanted to be sure that the taxes it granted would, when collected, be used to full and proper advantage. Particularly on the latter score, there were times when parliament was restive, occasionally antagonistic. Mere consent to taxation by parliament was felt to be too elementary a form of control. And appropriation of supplies without further safeguards had become too familiar a gambit. It was essential that appropriations should be observed in practice. It was this which accounted for the Commons' demands for the appointment of special 'treasurers for the wars'. A demand for such treasurers in Edward III's last parliament (January 1377) had no result,[3] but a similar demand succeeded in Richard II's first (October 1377).[4] And the treasurers then appointed furnished written statements to parliament in 1378 and 1379, only to be then dismissed.[5] Nor was the device again resorted to until 1385,[6] only for the scheme then instituted to be so changed as to be virtually abortive. It seemed next to impossible to separate specially appropriated revenues from ordinary royal revenues accruing to the Exchequer. The natural tendency was for them to be amalgamated. And the government had other needs to satisfy—the normal governmental and administrative expenditures, including the upkeep of the royal Household—quite apart from the needs arising out of its foreign policy.

The Commons were especially keen that the government should conduct affairs at home as economically as possible. And, of course, it was resentment at what they saw as extravagance at court that prompted their severest strictures and led, for example, to the demand in Richard II's first parliament (October 1377) that royal Household expenditure should be moderate[7] and later, in the parliaments of May 1379 and January 1380, to the establishment of the commissions of enquiry into the state of the royal finances generally, but again with the Household as a special object of dissatisfaction.[8] Consciousness of waste was a chronic cause of criticism. Moreover, such criticism was bound to be sharpened when extravagant expenditure was believed to arise from self-interested practices and manipulations on the part of the king's favourites and other members of the court itself, men only too ready to exploit their propinquity to the young king as the source and only too-ready dispenser of Crown patronage. Criticism was given a keener edge still when suspicion arose that not only did the king's ministers condone the malpractices of courtiers, but even that the chief of them exploited the spoils system to their own personal advantage. Once the most important of all the king's ministers, the chancellor no less, was suspected of having consciously put himself in the way of enjoying an inordinate share of the royal patronage, and of having done so by underhand means, the way lay open to the savage attack on him personally in 1386. The king's liberality to his personal friends, favourites like Robert de Vere, was bad enough, but when one of the most favoured of those friends was the chancellor himself, exploitation of the king's youth and inexperience was felt to be past further endurance. Not so much

De la Pole's dismissal *per se*, as insistence on the dismissal so that he might then be open to impeachment by the Commons at the bar of the Lords, became an essential prerequisite to governmental and financial reform. More than malice against De la Pole personally was involved in his impeachment by the Commons. Their belief was that he was guilty of indulging, to his own financial benefit, in an improper exercise of his official power, misgovernment to which the king had been a ready party. And if the king wished to save himself, he must be compelled to allow De la Pole's impeachment to proceed.

Notes

1 For an eminently useful discussion of direct taxation granted by parliament in the decade preceding the Peasants' Revolt, see the new introduction by E. B. Fryde to Charles Oman's *The Great Revolt of 1381* (Oxford, 1969), xii-xxii. The period 1359–71 was 'one of the longest respites from taxation . . . ever enjoyed in the fourteenth century' (ibid., ii). For a longer account (as extended over a longer period), see Sir Goronwy Edwards, *The Second Century of the English Parliament* (Oxford, 1979), 25–40.
2 *Chronicon Henrici Knighton*, ed. J. R. Lumby (R.S.), II, 215.
3 *Rot. Parl.*, II, 364.
4 Ibid., III. 7.
5 Ibid., 36; 56, 66.
6 Ibid., 204.
7 Ibid., 6.
8 Ibid., 57; 73–4.

V

The Wonderful Parliament and its sequel

It cannot have been long after Michael de la Pole had opened parliament on 1 October 1386 with the chancellor's usual declaration of the causes of summons and demanded that parliament should make a staggeringly large grant of four tenths and fifteenths that, in order to be able to impeach him, the Commons demanded his dismissal. They are also known to have required the removal of the treasurer, John Fordham. The king not only scornfully rejected these proposals, but proceeded to dissolve parliament ('de consilio Michaelis', according to the *Continuatio Eulogii Historiarum*[1]). Richard himself left Westminster, the Lords and Commons, however, refusing to depart; and it was only under threat of deposition, communicated to him at Eltham by his uncle, the duke of Gloucester, and Thomas Arundel, bishop of Ely, that Richard returned and, on 23 October, dismissed the chancellor and, on the following day, the treasurer and the keeper of the privy seal (Walter Skirlaw) as well.[2] Immediately, their successors took up office: namely, Thomas Arundel, John Gilbert (bishop of Hereford), and John Waltham (hitherto keeper of the rolls of the Chancery), respectively. And, no doubt forthwith, the Commons proceeded with De la Pole's impeachment. But this was not all that the king had to contend with.

It was not long[3] before Richard was driven to commission, 'by assent of parliament' and in letters patent issued on 19 November, a 'great and continual Council' which, in addition to the recently appointed three chief ministers, comprised Archbishops Courtenay and Neville, Bishops Wykeham and

Brantingham, Abbot Morice of Waltham, the dukes of York
and Gloucester (the king's only two uncles available), the earl of
Arundel, and three other peers, namely, Lords Cobham,
Scrope, and Devereux. This Council, invested with such
general powers of governmental direction and administrative
reform as would amount to a virtual "take-over" of the royal
authority, and granted the right to resolve any internal
differences of view by majority decision, was to act for twelve
months as from the following day (20 November).[4] But drastic
though this measure was, it left the Commons far from satisfied,
and in the final week of the session (which lasted until 28
November) they petitioned for further concessions.[5] Having
first asked that the appointments of the three principal
ministers of state and the lords of the new Council (appointments already made), together with that of the steward of the
Household (another fresh appointment evidently intended but
still in abeyance), should be 'ordained and established' in
parliament, they went on to request that the new Council
should continue in being, once the twelve months' period was
up, until the next parliament met thereafter; that parliament
should now pass a statute forbidding anyone at all, under threat
of severe penalty, to advise against or contravene whatever the
Council might advocate; and that both officers and councillors,
in order to have access to all administrative and judicial records
needed, should remain in London during their term of office.

Understandably, Richard was indignant at this renewal of
pressure. And his response to the Commons' petition[6] saved
what of personal prerogative and pride he could. The important
demand for the extension of the new Council's term—so
important because it not only obviously lengthened the period
of virtual delegation of the royal authority, but also, incidentally, would help overcome any reluctance on Richard's part to
reassemble parliament (where, moreover, if the new officials
and their fellow councillors gave a satisfactory account of
themselves, they might well be reappointed)—the king rejected
outright. As regards the stewardship of the Household, he
merely said that he would appoint someone suitable 'with the

advice of the Council'. But not only did Richard so far resent parliament's interference in this appointment of the chief official of his Household as to put off the decision to replace Sir John Montague, who had held the post since 1381. When eventually, sometime in January 1387,[7] the new steward came to be appointed, the choice made was of Sir John Beauchamp of Holt, who for over two years (since November 1384) had been receiver of the King's Chamber. So shaken, however, was the king by parliament's actions in general that before the dissolution he made a personal protestation 'en plein Parlement' disavowing all that had occurred that might turn to his prejudice and that of the Crown, adding that his prerogative and 'the liberties of the Crown' should be preserved and maintained.[8] But the parliament, too, was not without its anxieties as to the future, anxieties which prompted it to provide for its subsidy of a single tenth and fifteenth to be levied in moieties, the first at Candlemas (2 February) 1387, the second in mid-October following, the latter, however, only if the former proved inadequate and—even more significant of parliament's unease—on condition that the newly commissioned Council continued unchanged, and the use of its powers unimpaired and not interfered with.[9] And now to the sequel.

Richard's reaction to the humiliations of the parliament of 1386 was not confined to his resistance to the Commons' final demands, or to the formal protest he himself made before parliament dispersed. He continued to make it clear that what the parliament had done was for him an anathema. No sooner had the members gone down than he disregarded parliament's condemnation of his ex-chancellor to imprisonment pending payment of 'fine and ransom', and by Christmas was treating him with ostentatious warmth of friendly feeling. Then, early in February 1387, in order to discountenance the authority and standing of the new statutory Council, he left Westminster and, for much of the time 'gyrating'[10] through the midlands and the north, not only abstained from personal contact with the Council until just before its term of office was due to expire, but even held councils of his own. It was in two such meetings, both

of them held in August, the first at Shrewsbury, the second at
Nottingham, that Richard took up a more positive, and directly
menacing, attitude, it being now his intention, as advised by
Archbishop Neville (who had now withdrawn from the
statutory Council and sided with the king), Robert de Vere,
Michael de la Pole and Sir Robert Tresilian, the chief justice of
the King's Bench, to declare illegal the whole policy of the late
parliament.

The method adopted was to formulate a series of questions,
some bearing on the actual events of the 1386 parliament, some
hypothetical in form but arising out of the conduct of the
parliament, and to present them to the royal judges for their
opinions.[11] These questions, ten in number, all of them
tendentiously worded, were designed to result in plain answers
which would affirm the king's supremacy over parliament, and
to insist on Richard's own personal right to have exercised in
1386 those of his prerogatives which had then been called into
question, or rather dismantled. And, in fact, the judges'
answers, stated in every case to have been unanimously arrived
at, did what was required. The first object of the questionnaire
was to attack and dispose of the idea that the king could be
saddled with officials and councillors of parliament's, not his
own, choosing; more specifically, to invalidate the statute
establishing the parliamentary commission of 1386 (*alias* 'the
great and continual Council'), on the grounds that it derogated
from the king's sovereignty (*Regalie*) and prerogative. The
judges agreed that, because the king had opposed the statute, it
did so derogate. The next, and a consequential, problem was to
have them agree upon what punishments were deserved by
those who, in varying degree, had promoted that development.
Regarding this question, the judges allowed that those who had
assisted the passage of the statute, particularly those who had
urged the king to consent to it, were worthy of death unless the
king was prepared to pardon them. Punishment as traitors,
however, was what was undoubtedly deserved by the two
(unnamed) individuals who had been responsible for the
submission in parliament of the 'statute' whereby Edward II

had been deposed (the one by so 'moving', the other by then producing it), inspection of which 'statute' had first prompted the idea of a parliamentary commission; by those who had forced the king to consent to the establishment of the commission; and by those who had prevented the king from exercising his prerogative (presumably his right of rejection). Other questions concerned the general conduct of parliaments. And in this regard the judges answered that punishable as traitors would also be those who ever again presumed so to disturb the normal ordering of the business of parliament as to deprive the king of the 'regimen parliamenti'; likewise those who, when the king, exercising his right to dissolve parliament at will, ordered Lords and Commons to leave, disobediently continued to act as if parliament was still lawfully in session. The last outstanding problem raised by events in the parliament of 1386 related to the offence against the royal prerogative represented by the impeachment of Michael de la Pole despite the king's passionate obstruction, following upon the Commons' insistence that not only the chancellor but the treasurer as well (and possibly the keeper of the privy seal also) should be dismissed. And this matter also was dealt with, in two of the questions put to the judges. When asked the first—whether, since the king was able to remove any officials (including judges) at his own discretion and, having brought them to justice, punish them for their 'delicts', the Lords and Commons could impeach them if the king did not so command ('absque voluntate Regis')—the judges are stated to have repudiated the idea, adding that anyone who acted contrarily should be punished as a traitor. When asked the second of the two questions (obviously dependent upon the first)—whether parliament's judgment of Michael de la Pole was erroneous and revocable—the judges answered conformably, and as usual unanimously, although with somewhat less assurance: 'that if that judgment were to be rendered now [*modo*], they themselves would not wish to render it, because it seems to them [*videtur eis*] that, being erroneous throughout, it is revocable'. This, as a statement designed to reject that judgment, strikes one as curiously roundabout or hesitant. The words 'now' and 'seems' suggest a wariness nowhere else present in the judges' answers. Perhaps the judges were simply uneasy at recollecting a part they themselves had played as legal advisers in the previous parliament. But however this may be, and whether intentionally or not, they had at least avoided, in their answer as recorded, making explicit mention of the responsibility, for the judgment, of parliament as a whole, the Commons as accusers, the Lords as arbiters. But, evidently, that answer satisfied those who had advised and framed the questionnaire, and those who had attested the completed document. And both former and latter included Michael de la Pole himself.

Regarded as a whole, the questionnaire itself reflected Richard's own personal devotion to a policy designed to demolish parliamentary control of government as exemplified by the parliament of 1386 in its dismissal of the highest officials of the Crown, the impeachment of the most important one of them, and the establishment of a statutory Council imposed on the king. By the very violence of the royal reaction it represented, the questionnaire was bound to provoke a strong counter-reaction, especially on the part of those whose political initiatives had been responsible for the parliamentary events of 1386, and who had been declared punishable as 'traitors'. Not surprisingly, counter-reaction, encouraged by ineffectual royal resistance to opposition, was soon converted into that far stronger and more terrible outburst of anti-royalist feeling which erupted in the 'Merciless Parliament' when the Lords Appellant, with especially the support of the Commons, wreaked their vengeance upon the king's friends, among the foremost of whom was Michael de la Pole himself.

Notes

1 *Eulogium (Historiarum sive Temporis)*, ed. F. S. Haydon (R.S.), III, 359.
2 It is possible that Skirlaw resigned rather than was dismissed from the keepership of the privy seal, having held this office since August 1382. Consecrated bishop of Coventry and Lichfield on

14 January 1386, he had more recently, on 18 August, been translated to Bath and Wells.

3 It is possible that, when Bishop Arundel succeeded De la Pole as chancellor (24 October), it was already intended to appoint such a 'great and continual council' as was to be commissioned on 19 November, and even that its membership was under consideration; for all six of those lords who were named as personally present at the ceremony of tradition of the great seal were, in due course, appointed to the new council, viz. the two archbishops, the bishops of Winchester and Exeter, and the dukes of York and Gloucester. The coincidence is certainly striking.

4 *Statutes of the Realm*, II, 39–43; *Rot. Parl.*, III, 221.

5 *Rot. Parl.*, III, 221–2. Although the Commons' petition, in its request for the appointment of chancellor, treasurer and keeper of the privy seal and of 'the great and continual council', would seem to antedate the appointments of 24 October and, *a fortiori*, the commission of 19 November, its explicit reference to the feast of St Edmund, King and Martyr (20 November), the date from which the council was to act, as 'la Fest . . . darrein passe' indicates that the petition was formulated after then (i.e. between 20 November and the last day of the parliament, the 28th).

6 *Rot. Parl.*, III, 222.

7 *Polychronicon Ranulphi Higden*, ed. J. R. Lumby (R.S.), IX, 90.

8 *Rot. Parl.*, III, 224.

9 Ibid., 221.

10 The word 'gyrare' is used by the chronicler Henry Knighton (op. cit., II, 242).

11 *Rot. Parl.*, III, 233–4. For a full discussion of this topic, see S. B. Chrimes, 'Richard II's Questions to the Judges, 1387', *The Law Quarterly Review*, LXXII (1956), 365–90. May McKisack, in her fine contribution to *The Oxford History of England*, entitled *The Fourteenth Century 1307–1399*, furnishes a short but good account (448–9), all the better balanced for her notice, regarding the judges' plea of compulsion, that when Bishop Thomas Rushook, the king's confessor, was also impeached in the Merciless Parliament, one of the charges brought against him was that he had threatened the judges.

PART II

The impeachment

(I)
The articles (second, third, sixth and seventh) charging Michael de la Pole with dereliction of duty in the office of Chancellor

VI

The second article

(paraphrasing the parliament-roll)

This second article of Michael's impeachment[1] contained the charge that: whereas in the last parliament nine lords had been deputed to consider 'the estate of the king and kingdom' and advise how best it might be improved and also placed under sounder management, and then, after the enquiry was made and a report both oral and written made to the king, Michael had stated publicly in parliament on the king's behalf that the resulting ordinance must needs be properly fulfilled, the ordinance was not carried out; and that because Michael was the most important official involved, he should bear the blame.

Michael's answer[2] was to claim that the officials and other members of the royal Council had executed the nine lords' scheme in part, as at Cherbourg and Brest, where a saving had been made of upwards of 5,000 marks a year, and that, so far as giving effect to the whole ordinance was concerned, he himself had acted with all possible diligence. In any case, the actions of his fellow officials and councillors were called into question by the charge, and certainly the officials involved ought, in his opinion, to be associated with his response. However, should they or anyone else wish to saddle him with any peculiar remissness of his own, he would, please God, acquit himself.

The Commons, however, insisted in their replication[3] that, in view of the statement in his initial protestation that he represented the king *ex officio*, Michael's authority was superior to that of all the other officials. So much so that, even allowing that they were in some measure to blame, it followed that he himself could not possibly be excused. Moreover, particularly in view of his admission that it was he whom the king had ordered to speak in parliament, his obligation to put the lords' ordinance into operation had been all the greater. And since, additionally, he had not denied that the losses alleged had in fact occurred, they requested the judgment of parliament.

What the record says of the award in respect of this second charge applied also to the third and seventh articles.[4] Regarding all three, the king and the Lords accepted Michael's plea that responsibility for the non-fulfilment of the nine lords' recommendations was not peculiar to him alone; but although his fellow councillors were also implicated, they maintained that if anyone wished to impeach him of some specific act of negligence, he was bound to offer to answer such a charge.

A proper appreciation of the gravity of this charge obviously depends upon a knowledge and understanding of the particular ordinance referred to as promulgated in the parliament which sat from 20 October to 6 December 1385 ('the last parliament'). Curiously, but a fact perhaps not itself devoid of some sinister significance (the engrossment of parliament-rolls being a Chancery responsibility), the parliament-roll of 1385 makes no reference to either the committee of nine lords or their ordinance. It does, however, at least contain ample evidence confirming what the record of Michael's impeachment itself makes clear: that what had been uppermost on the agenda of parliament in 1385 was the problem of royal finance, namely, the need for measures designed to increase revenue and, where possible, reduce expenditure. Certain common petitions of 1385[5] had included requests aimed to do both. In order to augment royal income, it had been asked that certain funds of the Hospitallers should be employed to the king's advantage;[6] that ecclesiastics promoted by the king since his coronation might voluntarily concede such first-fruits as would have been required by the Roman Curia had they been papal provisors;[7] that certain lords should be given special responsibility to search in the Exchequer for all manner of debts due to the Crown, including any which might have accrued as a result of the papal schism.[8] In order to curtail outgoings, it had been asked that there should be a year's stop on grants from Exchequer revenue;[9] that the treasurers for war should make disbursements only as was proper;[10] that military officials, including the captains at Cherbourg and Brest, should contrive economies;[11] that royal knights and esquires in receipt of fees but not in service should seek military employment on the Scottish marches;[12] and, not last or least, that the 'estate' of the royal Household should be subject to inspection and reform, by the chancellor, treasurer, and keeper of the privy seal, not less frequently than once a year.[13] And all these requests, save this final one, had been approved by the king. But the names of the nine lords, and the ordinance itself resulting from their joint enquiry, were omitted from the parliament-roll.

However, thanks to the discovery, by J. J. N. Palmer,[14] of the valuable relevance to the problem of B. L. Harley Roll K 28, the identity of the nine lords and, if not the ordinance proper, at least those lords' report to parliament upon which the ordinance was based, are now known. The committee, for the representative character of whose constitution there was ample precedent, comprised three bishops (Wykeham of Winchester, Brantingham of Exeter and Fordham of Durham), three earls (Salisbury, Stafford and Northumberland), and three barons (Cobham, Scrope and Devereux).[15] And it was their 'bille' which, after being shown to the king, was, at his command, considered by the Lords and Commons.

What the committee of nine of 1385 recommended was set out in a document of ten articles or clauses, the gist of which is as follows. So far as enlargement of royal income was concerned, they advised the king that Exchequer revenues rendered by officials who accounted annually, revenues which were already heavily drawn upon, would be greatly enhanced if he was more careful in making future grants, and provided, too, that suchlike officials, e.g. sheriffs and escheators, were not appointed as a result of private solicitation, but were sound men nominated by the 'great council' and chief ministers, and in accordance with statute. It was also the view of the committee that the profits of the Hanaper (the fee office of the Chancery) would increase if the king took advice concerning gifts or assignments and about pardoning fees and fines; that there would be a rise in the yield from wardships and marriages if he was well advised as to their value by his councillors and ministers and did not make grants impulsively ('soudeynement'); that the income from the great and petty customs would be greatly enlarged if the collectors and their associates were appointed by councillors and ministers, not by private entreaty, and, depending upon conduct, were subject to dismissal, and also if they were resident and did not rely upon deputies; and that this would happen, too, in the case of the subsidy on wool and wool-fells if the same recommendation was made to apply to the customers, controllers and weighers. Then again, although it was to be understood that the king would occasionally have many escheats to bestow as he pleased, he should do so advisedly, especially taking into account the 'noble and honourable' grants previously made by him and his predecessors. And touching income from the alien priories, the committee was of the opinion that there would be a higher return if the king refrained from making grants to those who desired them for personal gain, and if he were to allow the farms to be fixed ('arentez') by his councillors and ministers. So far as limiting royal expenditure was concerned, the committee thought that reduction at home was possible in the charges of the Household and the Great Wardrobe, similarly in the sums taken annually by various ministers in excess of their customary fees; and that the annual expenses involved in the custody of towns and castles in the marches and royal lordships, as well as on account of the ordinance for the keeping of the sea, would be reduced if these responsibilities were undertaken by commanders appointed with the advice of ministers and councillors and not in such a way as merely to satisfy personal ambition or private request. Whether the 'bille' was strictly identical with the 'ordinance' (still not discovered) is a point which must, obviously, remain undetermined; but some correspondence between bill and ordinance may surely be taken for granted, and the correspondence was probably close.

As will have been appreciated, the 'bille' was cast in general terms. No opprobrium attached to any named individual, save only the king. Michael himself, however, might have detected something of a personal warning in two particulars: in the reference to escheats and the 'noble and honourable' gifts made of them by the king, the reversion of one of the most important of which, the Ufford escheat, Michael had secured only shortly before the parliament of 1385 met; and, perhaps more especially, in the allusion to the profits of the Hanaper, assignments on the issues of which were normally reserved for Chancery clerks and granted in only modest sums, but from which Michael had been granted, again very recently, the large sum of £200 a year in aid of his newly conferred comital status.[16] However this may be, the inference of the lords' committee's recommendations in their 'bille' is clear: there was ample room for improvement in the financial position of the Crown, and this was possible if the king behaved with a greater sense of responsibility, paying proper attention to the guidance of his chief ministers and their colleagues in the Council both with regard to drafts on the revenue and in the matter of appointment of local accounting officials. It was the king rather than his ministers who were being openly criticised in 1385. But what the 'bille' might seem to have implied, although it did not say so in terms, was that his ministers and councillors had not previously asserted themselves sufficiently in either offering advice that was obviously necessary or, if they had done so, not insisting on its acceptance; and in this sense the warning the 'bille' contained was for all of them as well as for the king to take note of. Whether or not this was in fact the case, execution of the ordinance of 1385 was left, not to any omnicompetent parliamentary commission such as was, to the king's anger, to be foisted on him in 1386, but to the chancellor and his fellow ministers and councillors, in other words, to the existing administration.

A year later, at his trial, Michael was able to say in his defence that economies in expenditure, estimated by him to have been as much as 5,000 marks and more, had been made at Brest and

Cherbourg. Whether or not this was as a result of the replacement in the captaincy of Brest of Sir Thomas Percy by Sir John de Roches by January 1386 and in the captaincy of Cherbourg of the king's half-brother, Thomas Holland, earl of Kent, by Sir William Scrope in February 1386,[17] remedial action had certainly been taken in those two places. For Michael's claim that '5,000 marks and more' had been saved at Brest and Cherbourg is plainly justified by the facts: in Hilary term 1386 the fee attaching to the captaincy of Brest had been reduced by 2,250 marks, and the captain of Cherbourg's fee by 3,000 marks.[18] This, however, as J. J. N. Palmer has remarked, is less impressive as an economy when, as appears, 'the entire sum was saved from the fees of just two captains, all other being left undisturbed'.[19] Indeed, by drawing attention to success in implementing the 1385 scheme for financial retrenchment only in part, Michael was as good as admitting failure to do so in other respects. On this score, negligence could surely be imputed. But the crucial questions in 1386 were: was that failure the result of culpable negligence, and, even if so, was Michael, as former chancellor, alone open to censure?

The Lords, while in their judgment accepting the idea that Michael was chiefly responsible, rejected the idea that he was solely to blame. If he had misbehaved, so had others. This, indeed, the Commons themselves had implied in their request for the appointment in parliament of a sufficient treasurer, keeper of the privy seal, and steward of the Household, as well as a fresh chancellor, together with different councillors.[20] That the Commons really meant new as well as capable ministers, events were soon, of course, to bear out: the very day of Michael's formal dismissal (24 October 1386) also saw the removal of the treasurer (Bishop Fordham of Durham) and the keeper of the privy seal (Bishop Skirlaw of Bath and Wells); and although the then steward of the Household (John Montague) stayed in office, it was only for the time being.[21] A new Council, too, was appointed in the form of an extraordinary statutory commission appointed under the great seal, its membership limited to those chosen by parliament, and its continuance for the term prescribed (eventually a year[22]) covered by the threat of annulment of the subsidies the parliament was granting.

Notes

1 *Rot. Parl.*, III, 216a.
2 Ibid., 217a.
3 Ibid., 218a.
4 Ibid., 220b.
5 Ibid., 213–4.
6 Ibid., 213a, ¶34.
7 Ibid., 214a, ¶44.
8 Ibid., 213b, ¶43.
9 Ibid., ¶42.
10 Ibid., ¶41.
11 Ibid., 213a, ¶35.
12 Ibid., 214b, ¶45.
13 Ibid., 213a, ¶32.
14 'The Impeachment of Michael de la Pole in 1386', *B.I.H.R.*, XLII (1969), 96–101.
15 The bishops of Winchester and Exeter and all the three barons were to be included in the parliamentary commission of 1386, which the king accepted with the greatest reluctance and to which he remained irreconcilably hostile.
16 No previous annual grant made during Richard II's reign had exceeded forty marks (Walter Skirlaw's annuity), save the 200 marks granted for life to Sir William Beauchamp, king's chamberlain, in February 1381.
17 Percy, first appointed captain of Brest in September 1381 for three years, had been reappointed for another year as from 2 February 1385 and was still in office on 12 October following, only to be replaced by 12 January 1386 (*Foedera*, VII, 332, 452; *CPR, 1385–89*, 72, 117). The earl of Kent, first appointed on 20 November 1384 for three years, was replaced by William Scrope, who, appointed on 10 February 1386, was to take over on 22 April following, again for three years (*Foedera*, VII, 450; *CPR, 1385–89*, 129–30).
18 J. J. N. Palmer, 'The Parliament of 1385 and the Constitutional Crisis of 1386', *Speculum*, vol. 46 (1971), 487, n. 51. The reduction at Brest was from 4,250 to 2,000 marks, at Cherbourg from 4,800 to 1,800 marks (*Foedera*, VII, 452; *CCR, 1385–89*, 50).

19 J. J. N. Palmer, *Speculum*, vol. 46 (1971), p. 487.
20 *Rot. Parl.*, III, 221b, ¶20.
21 By 5 February 1387 Sir John Beauchamp of Holt had succeeded Montague.
22 It was requested that its period of office should be until the next parliament after 20 November 1387, but the king refused to allow it to continue beyond that date, that is, sanctioned it for only twelve months.

VII

The third article

(paraphrasing the parliament-roll)

This third article of Michael's impeachment[1] alleged that: whereas the king's request for a financial grant ('la Charge') had been conceded by the Commons in the last parliament (1385) on condition that the taxes should be spent as they themselves had specifically required, and the king and the Lords had assented, this revenue had in fact been spent otherwise, with the result that an ordinance for the keeping of the sea had not been observed and, in consequence, many troubles had befallen the realm and were still like to do so; and that this was the fault of the ex-chancellor.

So far as the record of the trial itself goes, Michael made no special answer to this charge, or at least no detailed one; and so that source of information is quite unhelpful. Apparently, he merely insisted that his responsibility, as in the case of the second and seventh articles, had been one which he shared with his fellow ministers and councillors.[2]

However, despite the Commons' objection to this excuse, and as in those other instances, this plea in extenuation was accepted by the king and the Lords when making their award: Michael ought not to be impeached alone, but must be prepared to answer any specific charge levelled against him personally.[3]

The meaning of this third charge is, on the face of it, plain to see. Measures had been taken for the safeguarding of the sea, but these, especially in view of the threat of invasion by the French, a threat even more serious in 1386 than in 1385, had been inadequate; the reason was failure to implement the appropriations of the taxes voted by parliament in 1385, appropriations which had been made as a condition of the grant; and this failure was attributable to Michael's mishandling. As will have been gathered from the discussion of the second article of the impeachment, the parliament of 1385 had been deeply concerned about the state of the royal finances generally. The need for more revenue and less expenditure was so acute that the special committee of nine lords, set up to enquire into ways and means of achieving both, had reported in time for an important ordinance on the subject to secure acceptance before the parliament was dissolved. And, so far as more revenue was concerned, parliament itself made a grant of subsidies: a whole tenth and fifteenth was to be levied as early as Candlemas (2 February) 1386 and, additionally, a moiety was made due at midsummer (24 June). All this forthcoming extra revenue was earmarked for expenditure on specific objects: the duke of Lancaster's proposed expedition to Castile; assistance for Ghent in her rebellion against the duke of Burgundy; the defence of the Scottish border; and the safe-keeping of the sea. Whatever might be thought of Michael's special responsibility as chancellor, and whether even the Council collectively could be deemed accountable for the unsatisfactory outcome, must depend upon answers to certain questions: in view of the amount of the taxes granted, were the policies represented by the appropriations too costly, and the programme *in toto* too ambitious? Whether or not the grant was inadequate to do all that was asked of it, did the money become available soon enough?[4] Might not expenditure on some policies have prejudiced other more essential ones? Had the administrative arrangements devised to fulfil the appropriations been satisfactory in themselves? And, if not, did the responsibility for those arrangements lie only with Michael as chancellor, or even with the Council as a whole? If, merely, the grant had been insufficient in amount, it could be argued that criticism taken to such lengths as to involve Michael's impeachment was hardly fair. But first as to the keeping of the seas, a matter obviously of crucial importance, given the possibility of French invasion, the threat of which, serious in 1385, was liable to be more serious still in 1386.

The Commons of 1385, quite apart from their final demand that their taxes should be partly spent on the keeping of the seas, had already been showing particular concern over this aspect of defence. They had requested to be told who were to be admirals, and that their names should be entered on the parliament-roll.[5] Evidently, the king was not in any position to answer satisfactorily, and simply stated that he would appoint capable admirals with the advice of his Council;[6] and no names were recorded in the parliament-roll. In fact, whether or not the Commons' demand was implicitly for new appointments (and Sir Thomas Percy, admiral for the North, was eventually to join Lancaster's expedition to Spain as admiral of his fleet), the government was slow to respond. It was not until 22 February 1386 that Percy and Sir John de Raddington,[7] admiral for the West, were replaced in their respective commands by Philip, lord Darcy, and Sir Thomas Trivet, and the supersession of this latter pair (by the earl of Arundel) soon after the parliament of 1386 hardly suggests that they were considered to have been highly satisfactory. But if their conduct fell short of success, it is only fair to remember the difficult circumstances under which they operated, setting aside purely financial problems.

Apart from protecting English shipping in home waters and harassing vessels belonging to the French and their allies, the main task of Admiralty, in preparation of counter-measures against the impending French attack from Flanders and possibly, also by sea, from Scotland, was to control the ships that would oppose invasion. But first this navy must be commandeered and assembled. Such a task was always a difficult business, but it was especially so in the spring and summer of 1386. There were too many demands being made, simultaneously, upon the supply of ships. Robert de Vere, promoted marquess of Dublin in the parliament of 1385, had easily managed to avoid taking up his vice-regal appointment in Ireland in person, but by the beginning of April 1386 it had been agreed that Sir John Stanley of Knowsley (Lancashire)

should act as his lieutenant.[8] To this end, orders had already
been issued for the arrest of ships at Bristol and in North Wales,
Cheshire and Lancashire; and by mid-April Bridgwater,
Axewater and Chepstow were also being told to contribute.[9] It
was past mid-June, however, before even the musters of the
force for Ireland were ordered to take place at Bristol, Conway
and Liverpool.[10] How many ships were involved in this
operation is not known. Admittedly the retinues now to be
transported numbered less than half the company with which
De Vere had originally contracted to serve. But the delay was
itself inconvenient: the departure for Ireland too nearly
coincided with preparations for the departure of John of
Gaunt's expedition to Spain, and this too was delayed. The
collection of Lancaster's transports had begun as early as 25
January,[11] and towards the end of April, when the duke himself
had reached Plymouth (his port of embarkation), the vessels
from the Bristol Channel and the east-coast ports had mostly
arrived.[12] But this fleet was still defective in numbers, and
orders to supply ships were still being issued to both northern
and western naval commands as late as 23 April.[13] Not until 17
June, in fact, with the recent engagement of ten vessels from
Kampen in Holland and one from Danzig, was Lancaster's
fleet, comprising nearly ninety ships and manned by nearly
2,800 seamen, complete. Reinforced by a Portuguese squadron
of six galleys and twelve other vessels, it sailed on 9 July.[14]
Meanwhile, as early as 28 March, writs[15] had been issued
ordering vessels of over 60 tons burden to be arrested in the
admiralties of North and West and sailed in haste to London,
the writs themselves alluding to the danger to England and
Calais from French attack. All the same, the writs exempted
ships commandeered for Lancaster's expedition (as also did the
writs currently issued commandeering ships for the transporta-
tion of the forces for Ireland). Clearly, competition for ships
was excessive and, coming all at once, and especially in view of
the French threat, dangerously so. Not unnaturally, the
government was aware of this, and did what it could to alleviate
the situation. On 9 May the treaty made between Richard II and

Lancaster's ally, John I of Portugal, included provision for a loan of ten armed galleys which, intended to serve under the command of English admirals (at Portuguese expense for six months, thereafter at English expense), were to arrive in England before Michaelmas.[16] More important, on 1 June the Council arranged with Lancaster that, once he had landed in Spain, his fleet should return forthwith.[17] Having sailed from Plymouth on 9 July, Lancaster called in at Brest, where he stayed until 20 July, with the result that his fleet anchored off Corunna only on the 25th. After the landing, it immediately sailed for home as previously agreed and, given favourable weather, probably reached England some five days later,[18] that is, after an absence of about three weeks, a period of increasing tension. The Council's insistence on an immediate return of Lancaster's fleet was expressly justified on the ground that 'maxima pars navigii regni' had been ordained for the passage to Spain, and that intolerable damage to the kingdom might otherwise follow.[19] Fortunately, the French army which was to undertake the invasion of England did not arrive at Sluis, its port of embarkation, much before Michaelmas, and it was another month before all its preparations were complete.[20] But invasion had been long expected, and the English were not to know when resistance would be called for.[21] It might well have been more nearly touch-and-go. (In 1385 the French invasion fleet had been ready in mid-July.[22]) The parliament of 1385, in appropriating taxation to Lancaster's Spanish enterprise, had obviously approved of it. Parliament had done so when there was still a threat of French invasion which was likely to recur, and ought to have foreseen the predicament which Lancaster's expedition of 1386 was bound to create if its departure happened to be long delayed, as in actual fact it was. If the problems of naval defence in the summer of 1386 were increased by so major a withdrawal of shipping as was necessitated, however temporarily, by Lancaster's venture, this was certainly not all the Council's fault, still less the chancellor's alone.

There is another matter directly related to the question of the conduct of affairs at sea in 1386, one which concerned the Council but involved Michael especially. Evidently, during the summer English squadrons had been active on patrol in the Channel, and in June occurred a series of incidents the outcome of which further discredited the chancellor. From the commissions of enquiry authorised by the Council between 26 July and Michael's dismissal from office,[23] it appears that naval forces under the admirals for the North and the West (Lord Darcy and Trivet) and Sir Baldwin de Raddington, the controller of the royal Household, had captured in the Downs and taken into Sandwich a fair number of large vessels (variously called cogs and tarrits) which were bound for Sluis. Most of these vessels were Genoese, and two were owned by Piedmontese merchants from Piacenza; but they also included Spanish and Flemish ships, and all were suspected of carrying enemy merchandise. What the Council had to decide, of course, was whether capture was justified, whether to release the vessels and their cargoes and, if the cargoes had been unloaded, subjected to unauthorised seizure and could not be restored, whether to make monetary reparation. It proved to be a complicated problem, and some of the captured ships were still at Sandwich in February 1387.[24] Meanwhile, however, on 17 August the Council had informed Sir Simon de Burley, the warden of the Cinque Ports, and the admirals (or their deputies) that they were to allow one of the Genoese vessels to proceed to London.[25] On 24 September Burley was told to release the only Aragonese ship involved.[26] Then, on 18 October (when parliament was already in session, and only five days before Michael was deprived of the great seal), the Council ordered Burley to permit some of the Genoese and Italian merchants, on their professing themselves friends, to sell or re-export their goods, which, now alleged to have been originally destined for the English Staple at Middelburg in Zeeland, they were to promise not to take to Sluis or any other enemy port; their vessels, however, were to remain in custody at Sandwich until further notice.[27]

The arrest of ships suspected of being owned or freighted by enemy aliens was nothing exceptional, but the number, size and origins of the vessels thus captured by royal squadrons under high-ranking command evidently made a deep impression. Certainly it caught the attention of the chroniclers Thomas Walsingham of St Albans and Henry Knighton of Leicester. Both of them commented on the affair, and in terms extremely hostile and discreditable to the chancellor. Walsingham,[28] after briefly mentioning the capture of five great cogs and six tarrits as the work of the 'familia Regis' commanded by 'Dominus de Garsi' (*recte* Lord Darcy), goes on to say that, when the vessels were brought into Sandwich and unloaded, the Genoese hurried up to London to ask for the chancellor's help; that Michael, a merchant's son himself, and more interested in trade than soldiering, sympathised with them in their misfortune, persuaded the king to write to the captors to desist from spoliation and restore what they had taken, and ordered all the merchants' losses to be made good from royal funds; and that, therefore, the king had been deceived, the kingdom deprived of money, and barbarous and cruel enemies sent away in peace and well furnished. And, Walsingham concluded, no sooner had the Genoese left than they made for Flanders and entered Sluis. Knighton is not so expansive. In fact, of the captures at sea all he says is that Sir Baldwin de Raddington took two tarrits and, later in June, Lord Darcy took four tarrits and six large ships. But as regards the prizes first captured, he[29] says that the chancellor, having accepted a large sum of money, released them on his own initiative ('dimisit capite proprio') and by warrant of the great seal ('per warentum sigilli cancellarie'). And then he adds, very interestingly in the present context: 'et de illo in proximo parliamento [Michael] accusatus fuit per communes'.

The record of Michael's impeachment contains no reference to the subject of the capture of the Genoese ships and its aftermath, but it is quite possible that it came up in the exchanges between the Commons and the deposed chancellor. Walsingham and Knighton oversimplify a long and complicated series of transactions, which was certainly not at an end when Michael was impeached; and no doubt, in the light of the outcome, it suited the two chroniclers to exaggerate the chancellor's personal rôle in the affair. But the episode is a part of the story of the keeping of the sea in the closing months of Michael's last year of office; and, coming when it did, and given the circumstances of Michael's dismissal and impeachment, it can only have redounded to his disadvantage. And not only as regards his general standing in the public eye: if it was believed that he was primarily responsible for the Council's policy of restitution to the Genoese, it can hardly have added to his popularity in the royal Household and with the admirals, the latter having evidently wished to deal with the captured vessels as prizes.

We may now turn to consider the more important aspect of the situation represented in this third article of Michael's impeachment, viz. the question of appropriation of supply. As the record of the charge stands, the Commons were not here complaining of the government's failure to observe all appropriations made by the previous parliament so much as drawing particular attention to its serious neglect to apply revenue from taxation effectively to the safe-keeping of the sea. It is, however, possible that behind this charge lay dissatisfaction on the Commons' part with the mistreatment accorded the most important single one of the recommendations they had made in 1385 regarding appropriations in general. What had been then requested by the Commons was the appointment of two of the lords as 'tresorers de guerre' who, having been formally given their charge in parliament, were alone to authorise all payments made by subordinates ('deputez') similarly appointed, and to do so by their own special warrants.[30] The request is followed in the parliament-roll by a statement (in Latin) of what, however, parliament actually decided. Here the two lords were named as Thomas Branting-ham, bishop of Exeter, and John, lord Cobham (both of them members of the investigatory committee of nine lords), and their subordinates as William de Gunthorpe, baron of the

Exchequer, and John Hadleigh and Nicholas Exton (aldermen of London, both then sitting as members for the City); and all five were named 'in pleno parliamento'.[31] Otherwise, however, the decision taken by parliament changed the Commons' design, making significant variations in nomenclature and one other alteration of much greater importance: the statement refers to the two lords as 'surveyors' (not 'treasurers') and to their subordinates as 'receivers' (not 'deputies'); and although the latter were to make payments under the surveillance and with the assent of the former, their warrants were to be warrants from the king, meaning, any warrants which the king (presumably as advised by the Council) deemed sufficient. In other words, the authority which the Commons had asked should be vested in the two lords as 'treasurers' was reduced, and by parliament itself. No doubt the government had been very reluctant to accept the Commons' proposal as it stood.

This reluctance on the government's part was to show itself in other, practical ways. For instance, the writs appointing the collectors of the subsidies,[32] issued on 6 December 1385 (the day of parliament's dissolution), did no more than instruct them to account in the Exchequer or other place appointed by the king. Moreover, it was not until 30 January 1386, only three days before the first levy of the subsidies fell due, that letters patent appointing the surveyors and receivers passed the great seal.[33] It is perhaps not specially remarkable that Gunthorpe, the secondary baron of the Exchequer, who, an elderly man, was to retire from that office less than two years later, no longer figured among the receivers. Otherwise, however, the patent not only confirmed parliament's modification of the Commons' original scheme, but did so in such terms and detail as to clarify parliament's final intention, including a crucially intimate involvement of the Council and the Exchequer in the procedures designed to regulate the expenditure of the taxes. For what the patent stated was that parliament had recommended that the subsidies should be spent on the wars and the safe-keeping of the sea 'by the advice of the Council'; that it was to be the Council which was to 'ordain' what payments should be made by the receivers; and that, although the receipt and issue of all moneys was to be supervised by the two lords specially appointed, the receivers were to certify the Lower Exchequer, by bills under their seals, of all sums received and, at the end of each week, similarly specify all payments, producing also their warrants from the Council which were to take the form of privy seal writs. The immediate object of the certificates of particulars of income from the subsidies was to enable entries to be made in the Lower Exchequer's receipt rolls and allow tallies to be levied exonerating the local collectors. The weekly submission of particulars of payments and of all warrants therefor was something more significant, being directly related to the question of the responsibility of surveyors and receivers alike: such information, entered on the issue rolls, was expressly intended to constitute so full an allowance and discharge to both surveyors and receivers as would leave them free of accountability elsewhere; and by 'elsewhere' no doubt parliament was meant. This less onerous personal responsibility on the part of the receivers, indeed the reduction in the administrative scope of their task, is reflected in the modest fees the patent provided for their labours, for each was to have no more than £20. Well might Tout note 'the elaborate way in which the exceptional machinery for the collection and disbursement of the war grant was dovetailed into the Exchequer system'.[34] But what was most important about the instructions in the patent of 30 January 1386 was its explicit provision for conciliar control over the receivers' activities, for this had the obvious effect of reducing the surveyors, whom the Commons had wished to invest with powers of decision over payments, to only a minor rôle. Indeed, coupled with the arrangements of 30 January for the accountability of the receivers to the Exchequer, the Council's powers of decision over payments (as expressed in their warrants) made the surveyors little short of redundant, something of an administrative anomaly.

Evidently the Commons' proposals in 1385 for ensuring an effective appropriation of supply had fallen far short of acceptance. But this was parliament's own doing. If the government had raised objections, these can only have been thought valid by the Lords. Certainly, parliament had preferred not to leave the prime responsibility for disbursement of the subsidies to 'treasurers for war' as the Commons had requested; rather, it had sanctioned use of warrants from the king (witness the parliament-roll) *alias* Council warrants (witness the letters patent of 30 January 1386). Although taking up the Commons' scheme so far as to appoint special agents, i.e. 'surveyors' and 'receivers', parliament had virtually emasculated it. And if the Commons, when impeaching Michael, were not only complaining of the misapplication of the subsidies voted in 1385 but also, as is possible, treating the modification of their original scheme for controlling expenditure as a contributory factor, this was because they were choosing to ignore or disregard the responsibility of parliament as a whole for what had occurred. But why had the parliament of 1385 finally decided to act in this way? After all, the device of special treasurers and/or receivers was nothing new. But, then, under what conditions, and with what success, had it previously operated? Had earlier experience shown such a device to be administratively workable, or had it been only of doubtful utility?

Although the device was not new in 1385, its history was then only a short one. Not until Edward III's last parliament (January 1377) had the Commons first requested its use.[35] They then asked for the appointment of two earls and two barons as 'gardeins et tresoriers' who, being entrusted with the proceeds of the wool subsidies voted in 1376, of the poll tax the Commons had just granted, and of a clerical subsidy they anticipated, would undertake on oath to spend all these moneys only on the war; but then, realising the cost in wages of these special treasurers for war, the Commons dropped the idea. However, in Richard II's first parliament (October 1377) they reverted to it; and it was then decided[36] to consign all the above-mentioned taxes, together with two newly granted tenths and fifteenths, to William Walworth and John Philipot (M.P.s for London), who were given the same title and responsibility and took the oath in parliament. Their patent of appointment,[37] issued on 14 December 1377 (a week or so after parliament's dissolution), allowed them for their labour 100 marks a year each, plus expenses if the business took them out of London. The patent stipulated that the special treasurers' accruals should be certified to the Lower Exchequer for entry in the receipt rolls and, most important, their payments were to be as authorised by the Council in writs under the privy seal. Despite the fact that, in the government's acceptance of the grant in 1377, the 'ancient custom' on wool had been expressly excluded from the treasurers' revenues, there was evidently some confusion over this, and it was the Council which, on 10 October 1378, confirmed the original stipulation, instructing the Exchequer to assign income from that particular source to the Household and other strictly royal expenses.[38] Only ten days later parliament met at Gloucester. There, in response to the Commons' criticisms and a refusal to vote more direct taxation, the steward of the Household, Richard lord Scrope, acting as spokesman for the Council, under protest allowed Walworth to furnish a written statement of account of receipts and payments.[39] This statement did not entirely satisfy the Commons, for they then went on to object to expenditure (amounting to about £46,000) on the upkeep of strongholds overseas and on foreign embassies, etc. Even so, they said that they were in favour of retaining special treasurers[40] and, although they did not name Walworth and Philipot, these two continued to serve. By 12 February 1379 they had an acquittance for their receipts up to 4 February, by when these amounted to £145,651-odd and had all been spent.[41] During the parliament of April–May 1379 the two treasurers submitted written accounts of what they had received and spent since the Gloucester parliament (following a voluntary offer by Lord Scrope on this occasion that this should be done).[42] But then the Commons requested their discharge, and that the treasurer of the Exchequer should take over all the moneys they still had in hand, and also receive the income from future grants.[43] In other words, the Commons now asked for a return to normal practice. The request was granted, responsibility being assigned to the Lower Exchequer.[44] No fresh 'treasurers for war' were appointed to take charge of the then extended wool subsidy or the proceeds of the new poll tax; and when the next parliament met, in January 1380, what was said by Lord Scrope, who was now chancellor, was that a clear statement of the yield of the wool subsidy and the poll tax of 1379, and of how the money had been spent, would be supplied by the chief ministers and other members of the Council whenever demanded.[45] After this had been done and the Commons had asked for the discharge of the then councillors, they further requested the appointment of a commission of enquiry, comprising not only prelates and magnates, but also three knights of the shire and three other members, the latter including Walworth and Philipot. The terms of reference of this commission, which was allowed, required (*inter alia*) a scrutiny of receipts and payments for the defence of the realm ever since the king's coronation, whether on the part of the 'treasurers for war' or of the treasurer of the Exchequer, and, regarding this and all else, a report of defects to the king and Council. Obviously, the device of 'treasurers for war' had proved no sovereign remedy and, so far as the appropriation of the whole yield of a grant of *direct* taxation is concerned, it was not again resorted to until 1385. Admittedly, when the Commons, in the same first parliament of 1380, granted one and a half tenths and fifteenths, all to be levied by 23 April 1380, and requested that this tax and what the clergy would vote, together with all arrears of recent grants (including the poll taxes of 1377 and 1379), should be applied exclusively in aid of Thomas of Woodstock's impending expedition to Brittany, they also asked for the appointment by royal commission of 'une suffisante persone' who, to prevent the proceeds from being confused ('medlez') with other royal revenue, should 'have their custody and administration and only make payments warranted by writs under the great or the privy seal'.[46] But no such individual was either named in the parliament-roll or formally appointed. Moreover, when, on 1

June following, it was decided to entrust to a committee
(consisting of a chamberlain of the Exchequer, the treasurer of
the Exchequer's clerk, Sir John Gildsburgh (the ex-Speaker),
John Philipot, and the English factor of the Florentine banking
firm of the Bardi) the full amount of what Woodstock and his
captains were entitled to receive as wages for half a quarter's
service,[47] this was of course a fixed sum, and in any case it was
to be taken from the proceeds of a clerical tenth leviable at
midsummer (viz. £10,000) and by means of assignments (for
£4,592-odd) on the wool subsidies at London, Boston and
Hull,[48] not from the one and a half tenths and fifteenths voted
by the parliament. Nor, at the Northampton parliament in
December 1380, did a request for 'treasurers for war' or
'receivers' accompany the grant of the famous triple poll tax,
although, again, the Commons asked for its exclusive appropriation to the fulfilment of the contracts for service in Brittany
agreed with Woodstock and to the safe-keeping of the sea. The
official response to this petition was simply that the money
would be spent with the advice of the magnates and the
Council.[49]

When, in the first of the two parliaments of 1382, the device
of special custodians of proceeds of taxation was revived, it was
not 'treasurers' who were appointed, with a commission to
control expenditure on war and defence in general (as had been
the case with Walworth and Philipot in 1377–9), but 'receivers'
whose sole function would be to provide for the safe-keeping of
the sea. These 'receivers', moreover, were to do this out of the
revenue from a form of indirect taxation not previously laid
under special contribution for that purpose, viz. the subsidy of
tunnage and poundage. It had first been decided that
expenditure on defence, including the maintenance of towns
and fortresses overseas, should be met out of revenue from the
wool subsidy, and that such expenditure should be left to the
Council to control. However, so far as the keeping of the sea was
concerned, an offer from 'les Mariners del West' to supply a
naval force ('armee') from then until Michaelmas 1384
prompted a separate decision to apply all proceeds of tunnage

and poundage during that period exclusively to that aspect of defence; and parliament then chose Sir John Philipot (M.P. for London) as 'resceivour et gardein' along the coast east of Southampton and north to the Tweed and, jointly to fill the similar office for Southampton and to the west, John Polymond (M.P. for Southampton) and Thomas Beaupyne of Bristol (M.P. for Gloucester).[50] Within a month of the dissolution of the parliament, on 18 June 1382, the receivers, now described as 'principal receivers', were formally appointed by patent, Hugh Fastolf of Great Yarmouth being now associated with Philipot; and the fee of each receiver was fixed at 100 marks a year, with a daily wage of one mark. The receivers were to take order for the necessary supply of ships and crews, which, once at sea, were naturally to be under the command of the admirals for the North and West (Lord Fitzwalter and Sir John Roches, respectively).[51] At the same time Polymond and Beaupyne were given permission to raise loans; and, on 1 July, expressly in order to expedite action at sea, they were even authorised to farm out the collection of tunnage and poundage in their area, provided that the farms, which in this western command amounted to just over £1,000 (1,540 marks), were paid in advance.[52] This latter arrangement, to farm out collection, had its drawbacks. For instance, in May 1383 the farmer of the subsidy between Southampton and Melcombe, William Bacon, was to have his grant of the right to farm revoked, on grounds of fraud.[53] But the scheme as a whole was evidently found difficult to work in other and more important respects, certainly so far as the Narrows and the east coast were concerned. For when Philipot and Fastolf, whether officially regarded as unsatisfactory or feeling personally discontented, were discharged by the Council within six months of their appointment and, on 15 November 1382, Sir Robert Assheton, the warden of the Cinque Ports, and Lord Fitzwalter, the admiral for the North, replaced them as 'principal receivers', what had recently been a single, jointly administered coastal area (Southampton to the Tweed) was now divided between the two men: Assheton was to be answerable for administering the proceeds of tunnage and poundage between Southampton and the port of London (including Tilbury and Gravesend) and Fitzwalter along the coast north of the mouth of the Thames.[54] In June 1383 Assheton took over the function of admiral in his own area as well.[55] But evidently all these arrangements proved unsuitable and inadequate: not only had criticism of lack of maritime protection been voiced in the parliament of February 1383,[56] but in the October parliament of·that year native merchants complained that, although paying tunnage and poundage, they were having to look to their own security;[57] and the seamen of Scarborough, claiming to have recently lost ships worth £2,000 at the hands of Scots, French and Flemings, asked in the same autumn parliament that they might be allowed to exact, along the coast between Hartlepool and Hull, special tolls on fish *plus* poundage on general merchandise, in order to equip and man, for self-defence, the barge and balinger they had already bought on their own initiative.[58] Although this particular petition was refused on the advice of the Council and of the admirals, parliament responded to the outcry, if only after a fashion: confirming the grant of tunnage and poundage until March 1384, it reaffirmed its appropriation to the safe-keeping of the sea, only to alter, once again, however, the administrative arrangements regarding both the collection of the subsidy and the command of naval forces. Although a tripartite division of the coast for the collection of the subsidy was retained, it was now decided to change the geographical limits of the constituent areas, these being redefined as St Michael's Mount to Hastings, Hastings to Kirkley Roads (Lowestoft), and Kirkley Roads to the Tweed.[59] The previous similarly tripartite command of forces at sea was, however, abandoned. In future, command was to be entrusted, not to the two admirals of West and North and, sandwiched in between them and with responsibility for the Narrows, the warden of the Cinque Ports, but to the two admirals only. Moreover, two new admirals, the earls of Devon and Northumberland, were appointed, the former as admiral for the West on 12 November 1383 (during the parliament), the latter as admiral for the North on 2

December (within a week of parliament's dissolution);[60] and they, acting also as receivers of tunnage and poundage collected within their respective commands (divided, presumably, at Hastings), undertook faithfully to apply the proceeds of the subsidy to the keeping of the sea as advised by the Council.[61] The two new admirals remained in office for little more than a year, being superseded on 29 January 1385 by, in the West, Sir John Raddington, prior of St John's, and, in the North, Sir Thomas Percy (Northumberland's brother). In the meantime, however, fresh difficulties had arisen, namely, over the protection of shipping engaged in trade with the staple at Middelburg, and a special arrangement was now made which can only have worked to the prejudice of the scheme already established. Deliberately disregarding the decision of the parliament of October–November 1383 that tunnage and poundage should be assigned to the two admirals exclusively, the Council on 24 January 1384 gave orders to the collectors of the subsidy in the port of London to deliver 500 marks to Sir John Philipot and two other London merchants who were to be free to spend that sum, at their own discretion, on providing safe passage for exports of wool from London to Middelburg and imports of other merchandise into England.[62] The general problem, however, remained as intractable as ever; and in the very next parliament, the Salisbury parliament of April–May 1384, the speech with which Michael de la Pole opened the session once more drew attention to the need for measures for the defence of English shipping, referring in particular to the danger from Spaniards and Flemings.[63]

All the makeshift contrivances of recent years, the 'chopping and changing' by parliament as well as by the government in their efforts to secure an effective return from expenditure on defence, including the keeping of the sea, show how difficult it was to achieve satisfactory arrangements. What had resulted from the parliamentary ordinance of 1385, which the Commons must have resented in so far as it had fallen very short of their own demand, was only another failure in a lengthening story of unsuccessful attempts to take adequate financial and administrative measures to keep the sea lanes open and safe. That at least may be said in mitigation of the charge regarding this particular subject levelled against Michael de la Pole 1386. No doubt the effect of the news that the long-threatened French invasion from Flanders (and possibly Scotland, too) was now so closely imminent—witness the orders of 15 October 1386 for the defence of Newcastle upon Tyne and Hartlepool which referred to Charles VI's intention to invade with a large army at the beginning of November at the latest—was to produce such an increase of tension in parliament as to result in near panic. The substance of the charge against Michael contained in the third article of his impeachment, may perhaps be regarded as so much evidence of that highly nervous state in which parliament found itself.

Notes

1 *Rot. Parl.*, III, 216a.
2 Ibid., 217a.
3 Ibid., 220b.
4 Cf. the royal letter patent of 14 May 1386 ordering repayment by the Exchequer to the King's Chamber of a loan of 1,000 marks made by the latter to accelerate payments for John of Gaunt's expedition to Spain and for other war business, the repayment to come out of the proceeds of the tenths and fifteenths granted by parliament in 1385; and also repayment by the Exchequer of the loans made at that time by certain Italian, Catalan and Aragonese merchants, loans amounting to 10,000 marks, repayment of which was secured on the same subsidy and the clerical grant (*CPR, 1381–85*, 141, 147).
5 *Rot. Parl.*, III, 204.
6 Ibid., III, 213b (¶37).
7 Sir John de Raddington, who was prior of the Order of St John of Jerusalem in England, was probably related to Sir Baldwin de Raddington, controller of the royal Household (Tout, *Chapters*, IV, 197 n. 6).
8 *CPR, 1385–89*, 125.
9 Ibid., 131.
10 Ibid., 157, 163.

11 P. E. Russell, *The English Intervention in Spain and Portugal in the time of Edward III and Richard II* (Oxford, 1955), 411 n. 1.
12 Ibid., 412.
13 *Foedera*, VII, 509.
14 Russell, op. cit., 412–13.
15 *Foedera*, VII, 507.
16 Ibid., 524.
17 Ibid., 521.
18 Russell, op. cit., 421 n. 3.
19 *Foedera*, VII, 521.
20 Richard Vaughan, *Philip the Bold* (London, 1962), p. 49.
21 The French army did not leave Sluis until mid-November (ibid., 50).
22 Ibid., 36.
23 *CPR, 1385–89*, 164–6, 169–70.
24 *CCR, 1385–89*, 200.
25 Ibid., 165.
26 Ibid., 170.
27 Ibid., 187.
28 *Historia Anglicana*, II, 146; cf. *Ypodigma Neustrie*, 345. In another version of his chronicle (*Chronicon Anglie*, ed. E. M. Thompson, R.S.; 1874, p. 371), Walsingham says that the Genoese, on arrival at Sluis, killed some English pilgrims bound for Rome who, trusting in the friendship of those who had themselves been so amicably treated in England, and having agreed a just fare, had taken passage with them.
29 *Chronicon Henrici Knighton*, ed. J. R. Lumby (R.S. 1895), II, 211.
30 *Rot. Parl.*, III, 204b.
31 Ibid.
32 *CFR, 1383–91*, 114.
33 Ibid., 135.
34 T. F. Tout, *Chapters*, III, p. 396 n. 2.
35 *Rot. Parl.*, II, 364 (¶20).
36 Ibid., III, 7 (¶27).
37 *CPR, 1377–81*, 99.
38 *CCR, 1377–81*, 156.
39 *Rot. Parl.*, III, 35–6.
40 Ibid., 38a, ¶30.
41 *CPR, 1377–81*, 327.
42 *Rot. Parl.*, III, 56a (¶7).
43 Ibid., 66b (¶53).
44 It was only on 18 November 1379, however, that Walworth and Philipot received their final acquittance, in which their period of

account was given as not having terminated until the eve of Michaelmas (*CPR, 1377–81*, 400).

45 *Rot. Parl.*, III, 71b (¶5).
46 Ibid., 75a.
47 *Foedera*, VII, 256.
48 These assignments on the wool subsidies were supposed not to be revoked by the treasurer of the Exchequer or any other official. The arrangement was given additional security by the consignment to the chancellor, the treasurer, the chamberlain, the steward of the Household and the keeper of the privy seal, of jewels worth £10,000 as a pledge of full payment for Woodstock's expedition.
49 *Rot. Parl.*, III, 93–4 (¶30).
50 Ibid., 124 (¶15).
51 *CFR, 1377–83*, 296–7, 299, 300.
52 Ibid., 306.
53 *CPR, 1381–85*, 281.
54 *CFR, 1377–83*, 333.
55 T. Carte, *Catalogue des Rolles Gascons etc.*, II, 143.
56 *Rot. Parl.*, III, 146a.
57 Ibid., 160a (¶36).
58 Ibid., 162a (¶46).
59 Ibid., 151b.
60 T. Carte, op. cit., II, 144.
61 *CPR, 1381–85*, 360–1.
62 *CCR, 1381–85*, 364.
63 *Rot. Parl.*, III, 166b.

VIII

The sixth article

(paraphrasing the parliament-roll)

This sixth article of Michael's impeachment[1] was to the effect
that during his tenure of office as chancellor there had been
improper grants of charters and of patents of pardon for
murders, treasons and felonies, instances of tampering with
records (*rasures de roules*), and sale of justice. Special attention
was drawn to the sealing of a charter granting certain franchises
to Dover castle. So far as the other, more general parts of the
charge were concerned, Michael said little in his defence,[2] or at
least said nothing very specific: his simple excuse was that his
actions had always been pursuant to a warrant, and that he had
been entirely innocent of any ill-intent or conspiracy.
Moreover—it being understood that as a sentence given by a
judge might be reversed as legally erroneous, so too might an
unreasonable patent sealed by a chancellor be revoked, without
any personal penalty being incurred in either case—Michael
asked that he should not be subjected to any innovation
(*novellerie*), i.e. to some penalty never imposed upon his
predecessors in office. His plea was accepted: it was merely said
in the judgment awarded[3] that, if any such charters or patents
were found to have been illegal, these, but only these, should be
annulled.

In view of the special mention of the patent conferring
franchises upon Dover castle, it would appear that the
Commons felt most strongly about that one of all the offences
referred to in this article. What these particular franchises were
is not defined in the charge; nor even is anything said as to what

kind of franchises they were. All that the charge says is that the franchises had been to the disherison of the Crown and to the subversion of all royal courts and of the law. The charge did, however, reveal that the patent conferring the franchises had been sealed since the beginning of the parliament. This latter point at least identifies the very charter in question, a charter in which is supplied the name of its immediate beneficiary. The charter is clearly one dated 16 October 1386;[4] and the beneficiary was Sir Simon de Burley, the king's under-chamberlain, who had been appointed (for life) on 5 January 1384 as constable of Dover castle and warden of the Cinque Ports[5] and was, in fact, to remain in office until, on 12 March 1388, he was himself impeached by the Commons in the 'Merciless Parliament'. On this later occasion it was to be alleged against Burley[6] that he had contrived the sealing of the patent only by procuring Michael's recovery of possession of the great seal after he had been discharged from office, and had already once surrendered the seal. The truth of this allegation is, to say the least, very dubious: the close roll of the Chancery records Michael's personal delivery of the seal to the king on 23 October 1386 (a full week after the date of the patent),[7] and it was on the next day that the seal was entrusted to his successor (Thomas Arundel, who put it to use on the day after); moreover, Michael's own answer to the charge itself admits that, when the Dover charter passed the seal, he had been properly responsible in every way. What the charter had allowed was the right of the constable or his deputy to terminate all pleas of trespass and real and personal actions coming before his court without making any return (to any superior royal court where, conceivably, appeal might be lodged), together with the right to use writs of attaint. The former allowance provided, or perhaps only sanctioned, larger powers of jurisdictional independence; the latter involved an extension of legal competence into a different field. The grant, however, may well have been regarded as aggravated by other considerations: it was made on merely financial grounds, viz. to assist repairs to the castle; its issue under the great seal was warranted only by a letter under the signet; the direct beneficiary was another member of the court coterie, whose political influence over the king was under grave suspicion, and who, in any case, had been granted the constableship on condition that he discharged his duties personally (not that this was always practicable), whereas the charter allowed exercise of its concessions by a deputy.

Before the significance and gravity of this charge can be adequately appreciated, or indeed the charter itself be properly understood, we must investigate, in a wider historical context, the question of the jurisdiction appurtenant to the castle and honour of Dover. The problem posed was no new one: the court of Dover had long been a "trouble spot", its jurisdiction a source of irritation, discontent and controversy, in the county of Kent in general and among the Cinque Ports in particular. As far back as 1300, in the *Articuli super Cartas*,[8] it had been formally established, mainly to protect the freedom from distraint granted by charter to the inhabitants of the Ports, that the jurisdiction of the constable of Dover should be restricted to pleas affecting the custody of the castle; nor was that jurisdiction to cover 'foreign pleas' of the county, i.e. pleas arising in Kent outside the territorial limits of the honour. Evidently, however, it was easier to legislate for such restrictions than to put them into practice. Objection to the constable's efforts to extend his jurisdiction had been made as recently as in the 'Good Parliament' of 1376 (when the impeachment, on other grounds, of William, lord Latimer, the then constable of the castle and warden of the Cinque Ports, had offered such an opportunity for protest, by written petition presented in the name of the Commons, as was now, ten years later, being afforded by Michael de la Pole's impeachment). What the 'poor lieges of Kent' had been opposing in 1376[9] was the abuse whereby many who were not tenants of the honour of Dover and were technically immune from the jurisdiction of its court, were nonetheless ruinously distrained by its inferior officials (*kechepolles*):[10] they were being made to answer in personal causes of various kinds, including debt, trespass and contract, that were only lawfully pleadable elsewhere, that is, in the courts of common law or in the courts of lords entitled by their own peculiar franchise. Such practices, extortionate and in any case improperly 'accroached' or appropriated, it had been asked in 1376, should be disallowed. What had been conceded, in answer to that petition, was that the jurisdiction of the officers of the castle should operate solely within the fee of the honour, and that they should not make process by writs of *capias* outside the liberty of the Ports. Sir Simon de Burley was not one to allow any diminution of the jurisdictional claims of his office as constable, rather the reverse;[11] and when he himself was impeached in 1388, advantage was taken of this to re-submit the petition of 1376 to parliament[12] in almost precisely identical terms, along with a request for endorsement of the favourable answer given on the earlier occasion (which answer had resulted, so it was to be said in 1391,[13] in certain 'good ordinances'). That there was still difficulty, doubt and irresolution in 1388 is clear, however, from the fact that no categorical answer was immediately possible: the royal judges and serjeants-at-law, it was then replied, would need to be consulted before right could be done by the advice of the 'great council'. No remedy was found, or at any rate none that was satisfactory; and in the parliaments of 1390 (January) and 1391 the Commons again petitioned on this subject,[14] on both occasions proposing the exaction of fines for breach of statute (in the earlier petition that £20 should be paid to the king and twenty marks to the party aggrieved, and in the later petition that the amount of the fine should be left to parliament to decide). On each occasion, however, the royal response was evasive: in 1390 officers of the constable's court were to inform the Council of past practice with a view to a general remedy, pending which complainants were to sue to the Council individually; in 1391 only the latter provision was forthcoming. Not surprisingly, then, the problem remained; and, under Henry IV, public protest recurred.

Although the petitions laid before three consecutive parliaments in the early part of Henry IV's reign (in 1401, 1402 and 1404)[15] explained the situation at Dover along very similar lines, it would seem, judging from their greater length and particularity, that the problem had become even more serious than before (or at least that the grievance was now more acutely felt): complaint was made that the stewards of the court of Dover, appointed by the constable, arbitrarily entertained all manner of personal suits arising throughout the 'geldable' of Kent (including pleas of debt not normally even actionable in county courts), refused to admit essoigns, received pleas of covenant already pending in the king's courts (illegally awarding process by writ of *capias* when so doing), empanelled and, for non-appearance, distrained upon jurors drawn from parts of the county at the greatest distance from Dover, and determined pleas of trespass against the peace and heavily fined those convicted; and that, since the stewards, on the ground that their court was not a court of record, consistently refused (even when expressly ordered by royal writs) to send the 'record' to any higher court of appeal, none of all this was open to remedy, either in the event of procedural error or of mistaken judgment. It was also alleged, so far had the jurisdiction of the court developed, that whereas a single yeoman had once served as messenger of the court (*bodour*) executing its precepts, this function was now discharged by an esquire attended by 'cachepolles' (numbering seven or eight in 1401, ten or twelve in 1404), who made attachments by illegal warrant and yet excused attendance in return for extortionate fines, those persons who declined to pay being brought to the castle and made to stay there until the next meeting of the court in the ward of the marshal, who then charged them 6s 8d a night for their lodging. Each one of the petitions of 1401, 1402 and 1404 asked that the jurisdiction of the court should, according to statute, be restricted to pleas arising in the castle or its lands and involving not more than 40s, and that every steward or other bailiff who defaulted should be liable, following successful action for damages brought at the suit of the party, to a monetary penalty equally divisible between the king and the plaintiff (in 1401 fixed at £10, in 1402 and 1404 at double what was at stake in the plea) or to some other punishment at the king's discretion. The royal response to these complaints was as basically inadequate and unsatisfactory as before: in 1401 the castle was to have its franchises duly used, and persons aggrieved were to sue 'en especial'; in 1402 and 1404 the records of the castle were to be inspected by the Council, which was then to act as empowered by parliament.

From those parliamentary petitions of 1388, 1390, 1391, 1401, 1402 and 1404 on the subject of the jurisdiction of the court of Dover, it may be inferred (and their evidence sometimes, indeed, very clearly indicates) that after 1386 that jurisdiction not only remained unimpaired, but continued to expand. However, this development can hardly, then or ever, have been universally deplored. The court must always have met the needs of some people, even on occasion local persons, and certainly of those who chose to initiate legal proceedings there. Moreover, the royal responses to those parliamentary petitions all suggest that the Crown was reluctant, in this period, to limit the jurisdiction of the court. So much may be said in general mitigation of Michael de la Pole's offence. Any extension of the jurisdiction, however, was clearly unwelcome, and abuses associated with its exercise provided those who opposed it with both ground and material for protest. Formally to safeguard the independence of the court, as Michael did by allowing the patent of 16 October 1386, was bound to be thought provocative: what had, in terms, been sanctioned by the grant was that important feature of the court by which, in effect, were protected all the most serious of the abuses attaching to its jurisdiction, viz. its exemption from need to make return of its record. Upon this return depended all possibility of appeal against its judgments (on the part of litigants who either were dissatisfied with them, or who, if defendants, might well have objected to the jurisdiction of the court itself in the first place), and also, therefore, all possibility of their reversal. For Michael to have done all this was possibly unwise at any time. For him to have approved the grant in such haste, especially as it was made in favour of Sir Simon de Burley and at a time when his chancellorship was under general attack and his dismissal from office all too likely, was so inadvisable as to be inept, politically inept.

Michael's replication to the charge particularly relating to Dover was made only in general terms. Once again, he pleaded that he had acted upon sufficient warrant. He pointed out, moreover, that the grant had been made for the benefit of a royal castle and, therefore, to the king's profit, and that he himself had acted in all innocence (*sanz male entent*). He did, however, admit that the charter had passed the great seal thoughtlessly (*legerement*), and without his having sought qualified advice (*sanz graunde avys*). He had had no idea, he said, that the charter was illegal, or to the king's prejudice; had he so imagined, the charter would never have been sealed, or if sealed would soon have been revoked and rendered innocuous. The Commons, in their rejoinder, confined themselves to the comment that Michael was intelligent enough to realise that it was his duty to seek adequate counsel, if only to ensure that he agreed to nothing liable to redound to the king's disherison and the oppression of his people, there being no question of legal opinion not being readily accessible in the persons of royal judges and others. On this basis, the Commons prayed judgment of parliament. The judgment awarded, however, merely demanded annulment, as in the case of the charters of pardon. And on 12 November, before the end of the parliament, the Dover charter was delivered by the king to the new chancellor, Thomas Arundel, for cancellation, as a charter that had issued from the Chancery 'irregularly'.[16]

Use of the word 'irregularly' in the context of this particular annulment points to what we may reasonably suspect was really at issue in respect of the Dover charter. For the warrant upon which Michael had acted in issuing the charter had been a letter under the signet. Evidently, such a letter was, in the Commons' view, insufficient as a direct warrant for use of the great seal. And perhaps this was also the gravamen of this sixth charge as a whole, if only to some extent. Certainly, what applied to the Dover charter also applied to other letters patent issuing under the great seal, including patents of pardons for murders, treasons and felonies, to which attention was drawn in the initial charge, although, it must be conceded, it by no means applied to all of them.

Ignorant as we are of the occasions on which pardons for felonies could have been granted and yet were withheld, the large number of such pardons actually granted and enrolled on the patent rolls of the Chancery suggests that they were even normally made available on a pretty lavish scale. And if, during Michael's chancellorship, more than usual were allowed, this would not necessarily mean that the royal prerogative of mercy was coming to be employed far too indulgently, or that the official attitude to the punishment of crimes of that sort was becoming slack. In fact, while Michael was chancellor, the frequency with which such pardons were granted did increase. In the roughly six years between Richard II's accession and Michael's appointment in March 1383, there were issued over 500 such pardons (excluding those arising out of the special circumstances of the Peasants' Revolt), of which two out of three were for homicide. In the roughly three and a half years of Michael's tenure of office there were about 450, with about the same proportion of pardons for homicide as before. A proportionate increase in the total number granted, but not a dramatic one. What really distinguishes the two periods is not so much the frequency of pardons as the fact that, whereas between June 1377 and Michael's appointment the warrant for a pardon was invariably a writ of privy seal, it eventually became his practice to accept a letter under the signet as quite sufficient, although this was never to the exclusion of privy seal warrants. During his first twelve months of office all but a very few patents of pardon for treasons and/or felony were warranted by writs of privy seal; and it was not, in fact, until February 1384 that he first broke away from this previously uniform practice. (The first of such pardons to be warranted by a signet letter was also warranted by a privy seal writ.)[17] Indeed, the only two pardons for offences which included treasons and felonies and 'all sales of the laws of the land' and, in the case of one of the two, 'erasures and embezzlement of records' as well,

Xerox
pp 94-95
pardone

p136
(Holland
Cord)

pp200-201
M deb Pob Jr/
Stofford

offences specifically mentioned in this sixth charge of the impeachment, were both of them warranted by privy seal writs. The earlier of these two pardons, which was for all of the offences mentioned, was granted to Sir Robert Pleasington (chief baron of the Exchequer, 1380–86), and it was dated 3 May 1383, only a few weeks after Michael took office.[18] The second, which was for all but the last of the offences mentioned, was granted to Sir Robert Tresilian (chief justice of the King's Bench, 1381–88), and it was dated 18 July 1384.[19] That both pardons were, as has been said, warranted by privy seal writs might seem to weaken or even invalidate the argument that the real gravamen of this sixth charge against Michael was his readiness to accept insufficient warrants, meaning signet letters instead of privy seal writs. But those two pardons were entirely exceptional: they were the only two of their kind. And although *they* do run counter to the argument, they do not invalidate it. It was not, in fact, until about the time of the second pardon (Tresilian's) that Michael adopted, to any significant extent, the policy of accepting signet letters as sufficient warrants for pardons of felonies. Such pardons as were so warranted had numbered only a bare half-dozen between February 1384 and the end of June following, but *then* their number immediately increased, and it continued to do so. And whereas from July 1384 to September 1385 (inclusive) pardons for felony under the great seal warranted by privy seal writs still outnumbered those warranted by signet letters in a proportion of roughly three to two,[20] from October 1385 until Michael's dismissal a year later the reverse was the case, and in roughly the same proportion.[21] In the course of Michael's last year of office the signet letter had overhauled the privy seal writ as a warrant for pardons of felony (as in other directions).

With the appointment of Thomas Arundel as Michael's successor, the quite general practice of issuing patents under the great seal on no higher authority than that of the signet, i.e. 'without the intermediate link of a warrant of privy seal' (Tout),[22] was abruptly discontinued.[23] And this applied, of course, to pardons for felony. Indeed, on 4 February 1389 (while Arundel was still chancellor) a pardon for felonies and trespasses granted on 8 January 1386 had to be renewed, expressly because originally sealed in the Chancery solely on the warrant of a signet letter.[24] In the meantime, during the 'Merciless Parliament', the Commons had complained of use of the signet to the disturbance of the law;[25] and subsequently, in January 1390, the Commons were to secure acceptance of their petition that no charter of pardon for treason or felony should, where the king's prerogative of mercy was involved, issue from the Chancery without a warrant of privy seal (any signet letter warranting use of the privy seal for such a purpose being obligatorily endorsed by the chamberlain or the under-chamberlain).[26] It only needs to add that when Richard II, during his Irish campaign of 1394–5, resumed effective employment of the signet and, after his return to England, continued with its use, it was only as a means of authenticating his private correspondence and not, as previously when Michael de la Pole had been chancellor, as a direct warrant for charters and letters issued under the great seal. Of course, the circumstances in which Richard ruled autocratically in his latest years no longer necessitated use of the signet as 'a special engine of prerogative' (Tout),[27] as had been the case prior to the crisis of 1386, when Michael's policy had been one of complaisance and compliance.

Notes

1　*Rot. Parl.*, III, 216b.
2　Ibid., 218a.
3　Ibid., 220b.
4　*CPR, 1385–89*, 225.
5　Ibid., *1381–85*, 366–7.
6　*Rot. Parl.*, III, 242a.
7　CCR, *1385–89*, 271.
8　*Statutes of the Realm*, I, 139 (28 Edw. I, c. vii).
9　*Rot. Parl.*, II, 346a.
10　By 'kechepolles', clearly 'catchpolls' (cf. p. 91) is meant: minor officials who made arrests for debt (analogous to bum- bailiffs).
11　In this connexion, it is worth noting that when, on 28 June 1386,

fresh commissioners of the peace were appointed for Kent, the opportunity was taken to make other changes: (1) the quorum, which previously had numbered nine, was reduced to one, this single member of the quorum now being the constable of Dover castle, i.e. Sir Simon de Burley; and (2) for Roger Wigmore (who only happened to be the deputy-constable just then) was substituted, the constable's 'lieutenant' without his being named, thus making the deputy-constable, whoever he was, a j.p. for Kent *ex officio*. (*Chaucer Life-Records*, ed. M. M. Crow and C. C. Olson, Oxford, 1966, 354).

12 Ibid., III, 256a.
13 Ibid., 290b.
14 Ibid., 265a, 290b.
15 Ibid., 476–7, 505, 540.
16 *CPR, 1385–89*, 225.
17 Ibid., *1381–85*, 381.
18 Ibid., 272. Pleasington's pardon was granted at the request of John of Gaunt, whom, earlier in Richard II's reign, he had served as chief baron of the ducal exchequer at Lancaster and as chief steward of Lancashire (a post he voluntarily relinquished in December 1382 (R. Somerville, *History of the Duchy of Lancaster*, I. (London, 1953), 484, 372). Dismissed as chief judicial official of the court of Exchequer in November 1386, Pleasington soon 'turned coat' and at the beginning of the Merciless Parliament in February 1388 accepted the rôle of 'mouthpiece' of the Lords Appellant (Tout, *Chapters*, III, 431).
19 *CPR, 1381–85*, 440.
20 In absolute terms, by seventy-five to fifty-four.
21 By seventy-four to fifty.
22 *Chapters*, V, 206.
23 Anthony Tuck, *Richard II and the English Nobility* (London, 1973), 70.
24 CPR, *1388–92*, 4.
25 *Rot. Parl.*, III, 247b.
26 Ibid., 268.
27 *Chapters*, V, 226.

IX

The seventh article

The seventh (and final) article of Michael's impeachment[1] stated that whereas an ordinance had been made in the last parliament (1385) on behalf of the town of Ghent, authorising the government to borrow 10,000 marks and incur a loss of 3,000 marks as the required interest on the loan, and this was done, Ghent had been lost all the same; and that this unfortunate outcome was due to Michael's negligence and mistakes (*defaut*). The record of the trial provides no explanation on Michael's part for either the loss of the town or the alleged waste of the money, although he could doubtless have supplied reasons, or at least excuses. All the record says is that because other officials and fellow members of the Council, too, had been involved, and he himself was therefore not alone responsible, he thought that they should join him in answering;[2] and that this plea seemed reasonable to the king and the Lords.[3]

By 1385 the story of the Anglo-Flemish connexion was already a long and sometimes complicated one. Given the old, and still close, dependence of Ghent and the other cloth-manufacturing towns of Flanders upon large imports of wool from England, the relationship between the two countries was bound to be of major importance to them both. Whatever happened in Flanders was of interest to England and, the county of Flanders being a great French fief, this was especially the case in a period of war between England and France. Before the capture of Calais (1347), any English expedition into north-east France had almost of necessity been launched from

Flanders; and it had been at Ghent that in 1340, although then partly to lend moral justification to the revolt of the town and her partners in the great urban confederacy of that time, Edward III had first had himself proclaimed king of France. Ever since, as sometimes before, Flanders (like Spain) had served as a barometer, registering changes in the pressure of Anglo-French antagonism. It was so, too, under Richard II. The Flemish revolt, begun in September 1379 and again led by Ghent, against Count Louis de Mâle, who favoured the French connexion,[4] was bound to attract English intervention sooner or later. Such a rebellion would at least cause great concern in France, and English support for it be an additional source of French embarrassment.

From the start the brunt of the revolt was borne by Ghent,[5] and between 1379 and the final suppression of the revolt in 1385 never a year passed but what the town was militarily involved. Ghent resisted siege in the autumn of 1380, in the summer of 1381, and through the winter of 1381–2. But then she resumed the offensive, so effectively that in May 1382, under the leadership of Philip van Artevelde as self-styled *rewaert* of Flanders, her forces took Bruges, with the result that the whole county was again convulsed. It was in this crisis that each side appealed for external assistance. Invoked on behalf of Count Louis by his son-in-law and (*jure uxoris*) prospective successor, Philip of Burgundy, uncle of Charles VI of France, French help soon came, under Charles's personal leadership and in strength; and although—despite the French army's capture of Ypres, its sweeping victory at the battle of Roosebeke on 27 November 1382 (when Van Artevelde was killed), and the capitulation of the rest of Flanders (including Bruges)—the Gantois refused to yield, 'never again was Ghent able to coerce or persuade her neighbours to join the cause' (R. Vaughan). It was in this situation that England, now fully recovered from the shock of the Peasants' Revolt, and (what is more to the point) greatly disturbed by the re-imposition of an earlier embargo on her wool imports into Flanders, but much more profoundly so by the prospect of Philip of Burgundy's succession to the county whenever Louis de Mâle should die, decided to intervene and assist Ghent. Only, when she now first did so on any scale, it was under the guise of an Urbanist crusade, led by Bishop Despenser of Norwich. Despenser's campaign (May–August 1383) came too late to help. Indeed, its general mismanagement led to a military fiasco and, following the appearance of another large French army, the English forces withdrew in a state of humiliating disarray. Despite the inclusion of Ghent in the Anglo-French truce, concluded at Leulinghen on 26 January 1384, and the death, four days later, of Louis de Mâle, whom Philip of Burgundy then succeeded as count, the Gantois still declined to submit. In fact, choosing to regard the recovery of Oudenaarde by Burgundian forces in the following May as a breach of the truce, Ghent again took up arms, only to be soon closely invested by Burgundy, a blockade in which the duke was assisted by his friends among the other rulers of the Low Countries, notably those of Brabant and Hainault-Holland, but the besieged by only occasional token supplies from England. Nor was the re-inclusion of the town in an extension of the Leulinghen truce from August 1384 to 1 May 1385 of much comfort to the Gantois: they had clearly been abandoned by the rest of Flanders, and, a matter of grave import, divisions were now opening up among themselves.

What followed, in 1384, was a development of which the consequences were directly relevant to the charge of neglect of the interests of Ghent brought against Michael de la Pole at his impeachment nearly two years later. For it was at this juncture that Ghent, only too well aware of her isolation in Flanders, and realising also the threat to internal discipline and stability, was 'induced . . . to alter her relationship with England from an association of equals into one of virtual subjection' (R. Vaughan).[6] Those still in control of the town now repeated an offer of homage to Richard II as lawful king of France and their sovereign lord. When made earlier, in April 1382,[7] a similar approach had been inconclusive. But this time Richard accepted the request; and it was 'tanquam Princeps et dominus superior' that, on 16 November 1384, he appointed Sir John

Bourchier as 'rewaert' of Ghent and (if only in theory) the rest of the county.[8] Bourchier soon joined the citizen-leader, Francis Ackerman, in the military governorship of Ghent, and in the course of the following twelvemonth received periodic payments from the English Exchequer for the support of his military retinue of 100 men-at-arms and 300 archers.[9] With this encouragement, and no doubt sustained by the belief that help from England would not merely continue but be heavily reinforced, Ghent again went on the offensive in the spring of 1385. On 31 May her forces narrowly failed to storm Aardenburg, but not long afterwards, turning aside on 14 July from an attack on Bruges, early on the following day, and with the help of a contingent of English archers, surprised and took the port of Damme, half-way between Bruges and the mouth of the river Zwin at Sluis.[10]

To Ghent this *coup* may well have seemed to open up a fresh prospect, perhaps even provide a turning-point. For the large French army assembled at Sluis during the spring, for a full-scale invasion of southern England, was obviously obliged to attempt the recovery of Damme, if only to ensure the safety of its naval base before proceeding with its main mission; and the Gantois must have thought that the English government would send the reinforcements upon which their retention of the port (and communications with England) so clearly depended. The English government was aware of the position; but although something was done to assist, the measures taken were half-hearted and quite ineffectual. A part of the French army at Sluis had already (in May) sailed to Scotland under Jean de Vienne, the French admiral, its purpose being to stiffen the Scots and help them with diversionary raids into northern England. And, in fact, it was this challenge from Scotland, rather than the needs of Ghent, that the English had elected to meet.

As between England and Scotland, the last twenty years of Edward III's reign had been relatively peaceful. Admittedly, the border, with its petty frontier warfare, was always a problem, and the English and Scottish marchers had been more than usually ill-tempered even before Edward's death. But the early years of Richard II had witnessed serious efforts on the part of both governments to maintain the state of general truce arranged in 1369, and a *specialis securitas*, 'a truce within a truce' (J. Campbell), had been concluded in November 1380 and, in June 1381, extended until February 1384 (when the general truce was due to end).[11] But the *securitas* was seriously infringed, especially in 1383; and in August that year Robert II of Scotland who, despite a prompt adherence to the Avignonese papacy, had otherwise held aloof from the Anglo-French conflict, accepted from the French a promise of 1,000 men and ample financial support in the event of war with England.[12] On account of the Anglo-French truce of Leulinghen from January to October 1384, and because Scotland was excluded from it, that promise of French help was not fulfilled either when, directly after the expiry of the Anglo-Scottish truce in February 1384, the Scots attacked, or when, in April following, an army under John of Gaunt's command retaliated and took Edinburgh. This otherwise fruitless English raid resulted in a new Anglo-Scottish truce, a truce which, although the Scottish marchers soon broke it, Scottish representatives at the Anglo-French conference at Boulogne, in August–September following, agreed should last as long as the truce of Leulinghen, now that this had been further extended until May 1385. Only then would the French be free to keep their promise of help, the promise accepted by Robert II nearly two years before. However, no sooner had the truce of Leulinghen expired than, on 20 May 1385, Jean de Vienne, admiral of France, sailed from Sluis for Dunbar and Leith with a considerable force (1,300 men-at-arms and 250 crossbowmen), and, in July following, this French force joined in a Scottish invasion of the East March.[13]

To the threat posed by the presence of the French expeditionary force in Scotland the English government's first reaction had been all but instantaneous. On 4 June writs of military summons were issued, and more were to follow on the 13th, all of them requiring the addressees to meet the king at Newcastle upon Tyne on 14 July. However, it was not until 20

July that Richard himself reached Durham, and only on 6 August that he crossed the Tweed. The English army of not far short of 14,000 (of which John of Gaunt was contributing nearly a third) had no difficulty in driving its opponents north. But, then, the main part of the Franco-Scottish force, which was under De Vienne's command, deliberately leaving the road to Edinburgh open, made an uninterrupted counter-raid into the West March. So damaging was this that Richard, after burning Edinburgh and quarrelling with his uncle of Lancaster about what to do next, finally, on 20 August, abandoned whatever idea of a major encounter he may still have entertained, and was soon back at Newcastle.[14] By 3 September he had returned to London. The whole expedition proper had lasted barely two weeks, and nothing of value resulted save a truce, arranged in September, and, more fortunately, disillusionment on the part of the French with their Scottish allies. The Scots, the French felt, preferred financial support to military help, and were ungrateful for what they had actually received from them of both.

But in one sense the French had succeeded: the Scottish diversion they had instigated had temporarily left southern England open to French invasion, and, moreover, had thus precluded all possibility of an English relief of Damme, where the Gantois were besieged by Charles VI from 31 July until 24 August, when the town fell. The French siege of Damme had roughly coincided with the English expedition into Scotland. However, that the siege had lasted just so long meant that the original overall strategy of the French—an attack across the Scottish border into England and, simultaneously, another against the English south coast—had failed of execution. For the French were now left no option but to relinquish, at least for the time being, all idea of invading England, and on 10 September, although not before his army had spread devastation in the *pays des Quatre-Métiers*, Charles VI began his return to France.[15] Ghent, so disastrously neglected by England, had saved her from invasion in the south when, given her heavy military involvement north of the Scottish border, she would have been hard put to it to resist. This fact was fairly recognised at the time: 'Se [Si] n'eust esté le siége du Dam, qui trop dura, le roy [de France] et ses gens eussent passé le mer, . . . et disoit-on, se [si] le voiage se fust fait, le roi avoit grant voulenté, puissance et gens pour conquerre le royaume d'Angleterre.'[16] Ghent, with little option now but to look for salvation in submission, had every reason to be profoundly dissatisfied with its English alliance.

When Thomas Walsingham of St Albans commented on the final outcome[17]—acceptance by Ghent of the French offer of peace—he spoke in contumelious terms of the character of its people, saying that, unwilling to wait for the help Richard II was preparing, they impetuously (*usi levi consilio*) surrendered to Charles VI, so demonstrating their inability 'to keep faith for any length of time to one friend or lord'. In the light of the writer's general hostility to both Richard II and his chancellor, such a comment might be considered a curious mitigation of the charge against Michael de la Pole. However this may be, Walsingham's sour accusation of betrayal *against* the Gantois is hard to sustain. Not only had the Flemish civil war now lasted for six years, resulting in a continuously expensive dislocation of manufacture and trade, but Ghent had fought the war itself with little interruption, and for most of the time on her own. English help, on the other hand, had been uncertain, spasmodic, dilatory, and sometimes (witness the Despenser crusade) had even done more harm than good. It is hardly to be wondered at, therefore, that, following the adversities and ultimate failures of the summer of 1385, a peace party among the citizenry of Ghent began to gain ground in the autumn. It was the boatmen and butchers who were the first to advise acceptance of Charles VI's terms, terms promising, on condition of a return by the town to his obedience, and of recognition of his uncle and aunt of Burgundy, a general amnesty and a guarantee of all normal civic privileges. But although most others, including the gildsmen and even Francis Ackerman, eventually conformed, leaving only Richard II's governor, Sir John de Bourchier, and Peter van den Bossche, the leader of the anglophiles, still prepared to resist, it was some time before Charles's offer was taken up. That offer, first made on 7 September, had to be renewed on 12 October, and it was not until 29 October that the magistrates formally announced their intention to treat for peace.[18] So when, in England, parliament met on 20 October, negotiations had not yet even begun. In fact, the Franco-Flemish peace conference itself only met at Tournai on 7 December, the day after parliament's dissolution. In the meantime, on 5 November, the English Exchequer had made a payment (its last payment) to Sir John de Bourchier,[19] and as late as the end of the parliament a message had come from Ghent to the king and Council, still imploring help and complaining of its delay.[20]

Certainly, parliament was quite willing to furnish the means of military assistance. Admittedly, its vote of one and a half tenths and fifteenths was chiefly appropriated to the support of the duke of Lancaster's expedition to Spain; and the claims of maritime defence and of the Scottish Marches, too, were formally recognised. But express mention was also made of aid to Ghent (*pro auxilio de Gaunt*);[21] and although the extent of this appropriation went unrecorded in the parliament-roll, there can be little doubt that 10,000 marks was intended, the amount which, as related in this particular charge of Michael's impeachment, parliament had authorised the government to borrow for this purpose. Indeed, on the very day after parliament's dissolution, 7 December, acknowledgement was made in Chancery of a loan, from a member of the Florentine banking house of the Bardi, of much the greater part of the sum required, viz. £5,000 (with security for repayment furnished by the parliamentary subsidy, supported by a deposit of jewels), the loan being expressly 'for the help and salvation of the town of Ghent';[22] on 11 December the mayor and aldermen of London lent the king £1,000 'to provide men-at-arms and archers for the help of Ghent';[23] and on the 13th the king 'received from a number of individuals a composite loan amounting approximately to £980, two of the individual items of which are recorded as being for the relief of Ghent' (N. B.

Lewis).[24] As the sum of these loans, '10,000 marks' is not far out. Moreover, in the meantime, only two days after the parliament (8 December), orders had issued from Chancery for billets to be made available at Dover and Sandwich for 200 men-at-arms and 400 archers, the retinue of Sir William de Drayton and Sir Hugh Despenser, who together had contracted to perform half a year's service (100 days paid for in advance) and were then on the point of leaving for Ghent.[25] But it was soon evident that all these measures, hastily contrived, had been decided upon too late, and so were worthless as far as the rescue of Ghent was concerned. Convening on 7 December, the peace conference at Tournai ended on the 18th, the terms including a renunciation by the delegates from Ghent of all English alliances past and present, and of all homages save to their lawful lord, Philip of Burgundy.[26] On the 21st the treaty was proclaimed throughout Flanders.[27] What little remained to be done soon was: on 4 January 1386 the duke and duchess entered Ghent, where they stayed for a week,[28] and then, on 15 January, Philip made a proclamation confirming freedom of trade throughout Flanders for all nations except the English.[29]

In the meantime, news that the negotiations at Tournai either had ended or were moving to a conclusion had evidently reached England without delay. In fact, on 20 December 1385, only two days after the treaty was signed, the force which a fortnight before had been preparing to set out for Ghent was ordered, now that that expedition was 'destourbez', to go instead to Berwick upon Tweed, there to remain, as a reinforcement to the garrison, for the 100 days of its pre-paid service, as from 15 January 1386.[30] So the force was not altogether wasted, and in fact did good service up on the Border.[31] And it must be also conceded that the parliamentary grant which stipulated the provision of help for Ghent was intended to finance defence against the Scots as well. However, so far as Ghent and the continuance of its revolt were concerned, such assistance as the English government had meant to make available obviously came too late. But, then, English external relations generally throughout 1385 were of no great credit to the government: Scotland had been invaded to no real purpose; and that invasion had made it impossible for help to be given to the Gantois when it was most needed and would have served them best, with the result that all Flanders was finally abandoned to the duke of Burgundy. Now, in the summer of 1386, while the duke of Lancaster was being encouraged to undertake the conquest of Castile, and before long was to leave for that purpose, England still stood to be invaded by the French. When this time the French again assembled their armada at Sluis, there would be no opposition from Ghent to frustrate their intention.

It can, of course, be argued that Michael de la Pole was only being fair to himself, and reasonable, in asserting joint responsibility on the part of the whole Council, even if as chancellor and chief minister he was its most important individual member. But all along Michael had been an exponent of the Lancastrian brand of English foreign policy, with its idea of opposing France indirectly, i.e. by attacking her allies, first Scotland and also, it being in John of Gaunt's own peculiar dynastic interest to do so, Castile.[32] In that policy the 'voie de Flandres' had had no proper place, and so far as Michael's part in its promotion is concerned, its must needs be noted that he had been all too ready to take the lead in the impeachment of Bishop Despenser in 1383, and also had consistently favoured the non-victualling gilds of London, the maintenance of whose centre of operations in the wool trade, the Calais Staple, involved if not peace with France, certainly a truce (witness the truce of Leulinghen of January 1384). However, it had been the Scottish campaign of 1385 and, in consequence, English inability to assist Ghent in the crisis of that summer which, more than any other single factor, had led to the final débâcle of the Flemish revolt; and, that being the case, the Lords in the parliament of 1386 could hardly refrain from supporting Michael in his plea that if he was to blame for the ultimate capitulation of Ghent, he was not alone in that. Not only Lancaster (who now, of course, was absent in Spain), but both of the king's other uncles and, indeed, many other great magnates had participated in the English invasion of Scotland, and so must be regarded as having been party at that juncture to the policy of which that invasion was an important facet.

Notes

1 *Rot. Parl.*, III, 216b.
2 Ibid., 217a. (De la Pole made this plea with reference to the second and third articles also.)
3 Ibid., 220b.
4 Louis de Mâle, although solicited by Edward III to give his daughter and heir, Margaret, to one of his sons, had ended by marrying her to Philip, duke of Burgundy, in 1369.
5 For what follows regarding the revolt, see the more detailed account in R. Vaughan, *Philip the Bold* (London, 1962), 16–38.
6 *Op. cit.*, 35.
7 J. J. N. Palmer, *England, France and Christendom, 1377–99* (London, 1972), 227–8.
8 *Foedera*, VII, 448–50. Richard II assumed this authority on the ground that Flanders had been deprived of comital government since the death of Louis de Mâle in that the latter's heir had not yet done him homage.
9 *The Diplomatic Correspondence of Richard II*, ed. E. Perroy, Royal Historical Society, Camden Third Series, XLVIII (London, 1933), 196.
10 J. Froissart, *Oeuvres* . . ., ed. Kervyn de Lettenhove (Brussels, 1867–77), X, 557.
11 *Europe in the Late Middle Ages*, ed. J. R. Hale, J. R. L. Highfield and B. Smalley (London, 1965): James Campbell, 'England, Scotland and the Hundred Years War', 207.
12 Ibid., 208.
13 Ibid., 209–10.
14 *Polychronicon Ranulphi Higden*, ed. J. R. Lumby (R.S., 1865–86), IX, 65.
15 Froissart, *op. cit.*, X, 562.
16 Ibid., 560.
17 T. Walsingham, *Historia Anglicana*, ed. H. T. Riley (R.S., 1863–6), II, 142.
18 Froissart, X, 568.
19 Perroy, op. cit., 196.
20 *Polychronicon*, IX, 73.
21 *Rot. Parl.*, III, 204.
22 *CPR, 1385–89*, 89.

23 Ibid., 74, 123.
24 *E.H.R.*, XLII (1927), 404.
25 *Foedera*, VII, 488.
26 Froissart, X, 573.
27 Ibid., 578.
28 Ibid., 579.
29 Ibid., 582.
30 *Foedera*, VII, 488. Cf. Walsingham, op. cit., II, 142; *Polychronicon*, IX, 73–4. That Ghent had 'adhered to the king's enemies of France' was certainly known at Westminster on 21 December, when, for that reason, the manors of Lewisham and Greenwich, which belonged to the abbey of St Peter of Ghent, were granted, for as long as in the king's hands, to Sir Nicholas Brembre and others (*CFR*, *1383–91*, 122).
31 According to the *Polychronicon* (IX, 77), the force sent to Berwick-upon-Tweed fought the Scots well on a number of occasions.
32 On the whole question of Michael's promotion of a 'Lancastrian' foreign policy, see M. V. Clarke, *Fourteenth Century Studies*, ed. L. S. Sutherland and M. McKisack (Oxford, 1937), 40–6.

PART III

The impeachment

(II)
The articles (first, fourth and fifth) charging De la Pole with peculation when Chancellor

X

The first article

(paraphrasing the parliament-roll)[1]

The first charge against Michael was that, while chancellor and sworn to promote the king's financial advantage, he had contravened this official oath by 'purchasing' lands, tenements, and other sources of royal income which not only were of great value (as was evidenced by Chancery records), but also exceeded his deserts, especially in view of the great needs of the Crown; moreover, as a result of his being chancellor when he acquired the estates, their annual worth had been grossly underestimated in the 'extents' (valuations), so that, it was further alleged, the king had been victim of a deception.

In responding to this charge,[2] Michael stated that he had not 'purchased' any royal lands since his appointment as chancellor (March 1383); nor, until the conferment of his earldom (August 1385), had the king granted him any estates save by way of true exchange. In this latter connexion he then specifically alluded to lands received in lieu of an annuity of 400 marks (£266 13s 4d) previously charged on the customs revenue of the port of Hull. This annuity, he maintained, had been his by inheritance; and part of the lands received instead of it had been transferred before he became chancellor, only part since then. In any case, the exchange had been to the king's benefit, particularly in view of a payment of 1,000 marks which he had made as part of the transaction. He went on to say that his creation as earl of Suffolk (a title vacated on the death of William de Ufford in 1382) had not arisen from his own desire or greed (*coveitise*); rather, having occurred when the king, during his first military expedition (the

Scottish expedition of 1385) and to do himself honour, had also created dukes and conferred knighthoods, it had been entirely of the king's own doing and at his behest. It had then been for the king to determine what endowment he (Michael) should receive to maintain his new dignity, and an endowment with as much land as had been allowed to his predecessor in the title was what the king had decided. Although it is not explicitly stated, in the record of Michael's response, that he was to have lands actually once held by William de Ufford, this follows from his next assertion: that he had pointed out to the king that all the lands intended for his endowment were held, for life, either by the queen or the late earl's widow (*la dame de Suffolk*); and it was for this reason that the king had undertaken to make other, equivalent provision, until those lands escheated. As to whether he had deserved such reward, Michael replied that this was not for him to say: yet he would say one thing, namely, that whoever brought any charge against him would, if it were disproved, himself deserve its appropriate penalty; and, he added, he had twice been a prisoner-of-war, and once, when ambassador for the king's marriage, he had been captured in Germany, on which occasion he had been in personal danger, had sustained bodily harm, and had incurred financial loss, misfortunes the like of which he would not now readily undergo in return for that amount of land. He himself would say no more as to his merits, but if the king wished to 'record' other evidence, it might be well that he should do so. Certainly, according to the record, Richard, lord Scrope, spoke up for Michael: how he had served as a knight banneret (*travaillé a Baner*) for upwards of thirty years free of shame or reproach, had been captain of Calais, an admiral and a diplomatic envoy; how he had long been chancellor and a member of the king's Council; and how, too, having been suitably and adequately endowed (by inheritance) and well able to support his previous status as baron, he had made no sudden transition from low estate to his present sphere; all of which, along with Michael's own reasons, might justify the latter's promotion to more honourable rank.

Following this intervention, Michael resumed his defence, reverting to the question of the lands he had been granted, more particularly to the allegation that, regarding their assessment, the king had been misled. His explanation was that he had personally asked the king to appoint men deemed trustworthy to see that the extents were made justly, only for the king to object that it would not be proper for him, as chancellor, to make new extents, and because also, should these prove the more favourable, it would arouse suspicion; indeed, it had been the king's will that he should accept the valuations of the lands made before his promotion to the earldom was ever under consideration, or he himself had entertained the idea (*quidoit*) of obtaining the lands. (Surely, no one could cavil at that!) Accordingly, no fresh extents, Michael said, had been made while he was chancellor, and he had, in fact, accepted the lands at their highest valuations, those most profitable to the king. And, finally at this stage, he added that his new rank, along with what the king had given him to maintain it, had been confirmed in full parliament, whereupon he had done homage, having been charged to do so by John of Gaunt (*Mons*r· *d'Espaigne et Duc de Lancastre*); and the king had handed him the relevant letters patent in token of possession, ordering the clerk of the parliament to include them in the roll of the parliament, which was done.

The Commons' reaction to Michael's response[3] was first to show the Lords a copy of the oath Michael had sworn upon the Gospels when he took office as chancellor. The terms of this oath (cited in the record) were such as to have bound him to serve king and people well and loyally; to do right to all men, rich and poor, according to law and custom; to offer true advice to the king and treat what was counselled him as confidential; not, knowingly, to allow the king to incur loss and disherison, nor, if it was possible to prevent it, to suffer the rights of the Crown to be in any way impaired; failing this, to inform the king clearly and counsel him loyally; and to procure the king's advantage in all respects, whenever it was possible and reasonable to do so. The oath having been read and understood, and with the facts revealed in Michael's response taken into account—namely, that he had not denied that, as chancellor and after being made earl, he had received the lands mentioned in the charge, and had even openly acknowledged taking *other* lands in lieu of mere annuities, so providing himself in each case with a sure and stable income, and without clearly notifying the king of his losses—the Commons went on to insist that even if Michael had received a part of the lands exchanged for the 400 marks' annuity before he became chancellor, he was at that time a sworn member of the king's Privy Council, and that after being sworn in afresh on appointment as chancellor, he had concurred in the exchanges previously requested and, accepting from the king the remainder of the lands in question, had so completed the exchanges. The Commons, therefore, demanded the judgment of parliament on all of Michael's response.

After the Commons' replication and request for judgment, Michael proceeded to his rejoinder.[4] Touching his oath, he suggested that if its terms were interpreted in a general or unlimited sense, no chancellor would ever seal a royal grant of royal lands or property in favour of anybody without contravening his oath. And because the oath did not mention that he himself was more strictly forbidden to accept royal grants than anyone else; and because the grants made to other individuals of different rank on the occasion of the (Scottish) expedition, or to others previously, had not been called into question or regarded as contrary to his oath; and especially, too, because both his own new rank and the grants in aid had received parliamentary confirmation, it seemed to him that he ought not to be impeached on account of them. Further, he affirmed that having taken his oath of office with the intention of keeping it to the extent of his knowledge, understanding, and capacity, he did not believe (as he would answer before God) that he had either contravened the oath or acted against his conscience regarding the matters in question. Nor, he continued, did he understand how, if a chancellor, sealing royal grants to lords in support of their rank or for other reasonable cause, had done so only in pursuance of a warrant from the king, such action could be contrary to his oath. For, in his view, the words of the oath binding him not to involve the king in loss or disherison related to matters of which the king was ignorant (as was evident from that other clause referring to the chancellor's duty to notify the king if rights of the Crown were in jeopardy); and so, once the king had been informed, the chancellor might proceed to execute a royal order without infringing his oath. All that affected his own promotion in rank, and the grant he had received, had been done explicitly by the king's command, with his knowledge and at his wish, and not, therefore, in breach of the oath. And so, again, Michael protested his inability to understand why he should be impeached.

Nevertheless, it was on the ground that Michael had failed to appreciate the implications (*l'effect*) of his sworn engagement as chancellor not to suffer royal loss or disherison, rather to prevent it and inform the king of its possibility, that an adverse judgment was found on this first charge.[5] Although he was the king's chief official, and thus fully aware of the king's circumstances and the country's needs, he had indeed accepted the lands in question. For this reason, and also because no confirmation of the grant was recorded in the parliament-roll (of 1385), it was awarded that the lands should be restored to the Crown. Michael, however, was to retain his title of earl and the annuity of £20 from the issues of Suffolk (which went with the title). Regarding the exchange of the annuity of 400 marks charged on the Hull customs for landed estate up to that value, it was held against him that he had been unable to deny that he had first requested the exchange when a sworn member of the king's Council; that he had admitted that, before the exchange was complete, he had become chancellor and had taken a fresh oath, posssessing himself thereafter, none the less, of the remaining part of the lands, thus corroborating the prior contract; and also that he had failed to notify the king of the disadvantage contained in an exchange of an annuity, which was of uncertain value because dependent upon customs revenues liable to falter or fail, for manors and lands, from which income was constant and safe. And so the judgment awarded was that the exchange should be annulled, and the lands revert to the Crown, Michael retaining, however, in recompense for the annuity (which had been his all along by inheritance), the mesne issues from the lands, unless these profits exceeded the nominal value of the annuity, in which case the king was to have the difference in the form of a levy on Michael's personalty (i.e. his goods and chattels).

As we have seen, this first charge against Michael had been framed in very general terms. The record of his response was something more specific, and directs attention to much of what was actually in question. What emerges is that he was here under attack on three main counts: (1) that when chancellor, but before being promoted earl, he had procured the conversion of an annuity of 400 marks chargeable on customs revenue into landed estate of allegedly greater value; (2) that upon his promotion as earl, he had received an endowment greater than he deserved, this excess being itself enhanced because of the undervaluation of the lands involved; and (3) that, the use of the undervaluations being deliberate, he had broken his official oath and practised deception upon the king. The inference was that he had criminously exploited his position as chancellor.

Regarding the question of the 400 marks annuity originally chargeable on the Hull customs, the record of the trial makes clear that Michael, although admitting receipt of lands in lieu of the annuity, insisted that the exchange had been initiated before he had assumed office as chancellor, and was merely completed once he had done so; that the annuity was already his by hereditary right; and that the transaction included special arrangements financially beneficial to the Crown. All that is later mentioned in the record is that the source of the annuity—customs revenue—was naturally (being revenue of a sort that was liable to fluctuate and, in any case, dependent upon the prosperity of a port) unstable and insecure, very

different therefore from landed estate, from which income
could always be guaranteed.

Michael's own evidence, as it stands, can be readily verified
from the Chancery rolls. The annuity of 400 marks had first
been granted by Edward III to Michael's father, William, and
himself and their heirs, on 30 November 1354.[6] Part of a
settlement which, on the face of things, was one-sided and very
unfavourable to the family, the grant was in fact the outcome of
a recent renewal of charges of peculation brought in the court of
Exchequer against William,[7] who in the course of the
proceedings had undergone imprisonment between 10 July and
20 October 1354 and again between 29 October and 7
November following. The annuity in question was allowed in
return for a cancellation of all Edward III's outstanding debts to
William, amounting to nearly £22,000;[8] in compensation for
William's surrender of a previous annuity of 260 marks
(charged on the Hull customs) and of all his interest in the royal
manor of Burstwick, in Holderness, worth some £850 per
annum, and in the Nottinghamshire manors of Gringley and
Wheatley (formerly part of Queen Philippa's dower); and in
acknowledgement also of the surrender by two other of
William's sons (Thomas and Edmund) of the manor of
Keyingham (East Riding of Yorkshire).[9] All the lands referred
to had first been acquired, by gift, purchase or lease, in 1338–9.
The annuity of 400 marks granted in 1354 had been made a
charge on the 'ancient custom' of 6s 8d levied on each sack of
wool exported from Hull, on the understanding that if the port
ran into difficulties, and the wool had to be shipped from
elsewhere (York, perhaps), the custom collected there should
be liable instead; and if there were to be any official stoppage of
exports, all arrears of the annuity should be paid as soon as the
embargo was lifted. Steps were therefore taken to offset the
inherent unreliability of the revenue charged, but that
unreliability had nonetheless been originally recognised.

When William died in 1366, Michael was his next heir[10] and
so succeeded to the whole grant of the annuity of 400 marks;
and on 17 October 1377, after approval of a petition which

Michael presented at the beginning of Richard II's first parliament, confirmation of the annuity was afforded in the shape of an order to the Hull customers to continue to pay it, including arrears since Edward III's death.[11] Michael's recourse to parliamentary petition itself suggests that he was having difficulty in realising on this asset. And that this even continued to be the case is proved by the fact that in the parliament of May 1382 he again petitioned for prompt payment, on this occasion, however, complaining that he had been told he could not enjoy Edward III's grant without making fresh suit to the present king, and protesting also that, to avoid being disinherited undeservedly, he was being forced to request to have of grace what he was entitled to by right. It was granted in the parliament that he should be allowed whatever writs to the collectors he demanded.[12] Nevertheless, despite the success of his petition, it was at this juncture that he negotiated, with obvious haste, the first stage of that exchange of the annuity for which he was later to be impeached: in return for relinquishing over half of the annuity (220 marks of the 400) he received letters patent, dated 23 May 1382 (the day after parliament's dissolution), granting him, in fee simple, lands and rents which, having been held in tail male by William de Ufford, earl of Suffolk, had recently escheated to the Crown when, on 18 February 1382, the earl died without issue.[13] The grant comprised a rent of £20 a year, previously payable to the Crown, for the castle and town of Orford, and the rent (or rather, in effect, a remission of the rent which would now have been due to the Crown) of forty marks a year payable for Michael's own manor of Stradbrook, where, *jure uxoris*, he was a sub-tenant of the late earl's manor of Eye, together with the manor of Benhall (valued at 100 marks a year) and its knights' fees (worth 20 marks), all in Suffolk, and the manor of Dedham (worth £20) in Essex.[14] The remaining 180 marks of the annuity of 400 marks he was to retain as a charge on the Hull customs. An express condition of the grant, and one to which, understandably, Michael referred when defending himself against this particular article of his impeachment, was that he was now to pay the king 1,000 marks for the villeins and growing timber at Benhall and Dedham. The Commons' article of impeachment had implied that only after Michael became chancellor (and was in a position to bring undue influence to bear) had the lands he accepted in exchange not been reassessed in accordance with fresh extents, with the result that, with their annual value left underestimated, he *then* received more than he was due. In fact, judging from other record evidence relating to Benhall and Dedham, the charge may well have applied in this respect to the grant of 23 May 1382: for Benhall, extended in 1382 at 120 marks a year (if the knights' fees are included), had constantly been valued, in the first half of Edward III's reign, at as much as 200 marks;[15] and Dedham, although when granted to William de Ufford's father, Robert, in 1337 estimated as worth only twenty marks a year (not £20 as in 1382),[16] was to be leased by the Exchequer in 1388 at a rent of £28 10s 4d, and was to be sold in 1389 for 500 marks (in a period when a ten years' purchase was a normal selling price of land).[17] Michael's annual gain from the two manors over and above their current nominal value may well have been some seventy marks,[18] or perhaps even between ninety and 100 marks.[19]

However, it was certainly after Michael's appointment as chancellor in March 1383 that, as he admitted in his answer to this charge, he completed his earlier grant, the grant of 23 May 1382. But, first, he secured clarification of what had already been achieved. On 15 July 1383 he was granted a ratification of his estate in the advowson or patronage of the Augustinian priory of Butley as appurtenant to the manor of Benhall.[20] Precisely three months later, on 15 October, he procured another patent which confirmed his right to both the manor and the advowson (the escheat of the advowson to the Crown having been disputed in Chancery by the late earl's feoffees, until a local jury found that the advowson had been a part of Edward III's original grant to the Uffords in fee tail, not a part of their ancient inheritance).[21] Then almost a year went by before Michael made his next move: what, on 3 August 1384, he obtained was not only a confirmation of the grant of 23 May

1382, but also a grant of the reversion, in fee simple, of the manor of Costessey (near Norwich), in exchange for the remaining portion of the old annuity from the Hull customs (i.e. for the residual 180 marks he had continued to be entitled to draw under the May 1382 arrangement).[22] Costessey, first given by Edward III to Robert de Ufford in 1332,[23] had been assigned as dower on 1 May 1382 to Isabel, widow of the late earl William.[24] What now, in August 1384, was agreed was that Michael should have the manor when Isabel died, until then continuing to draw the 180 marks annuity from the Hull customs. There can be little doubt that, quite apart from any preference for income from land as against income from customs, Michael stood to gain eventually by this exchange too. Costessey, when given as dower to the countess, had been extended at £131 8s 5d per annum, and this was the extent on which Michael's grant of 3 August 1384 was based. Already subject to a rent of £10 payable to the queen (as part of *her* dower), the income from the manor was now made liable to an additional rent, payable to the king, of £1 8s 5d, in order to reduce it to £120 (180 marks)—the amount of the annuity which, chargeable to the Hull customs, Michael would continue to retain but relinquish later on when the reversion applied. Then, not only would customs revenue again be superseded by landed estate as the source of this particular item of Michael's income, but, clearly, the income from the manor would be fully able to meet the charge his grant would impose upon it. So far, so good. But this assumes, of course, that the extent of May 1382 had been fair. Supposing, however, Costessey had then been undervalued. If that were the case, Michael would eventually secure not only a safe but a higher income than he was ever entitled to. And certain indications do in fact suggest that the extent of Costessey in 1382 fell short of the mark; and, moreover, that, if Michael was unaware of this in August 1384, he cannot have remained in ignorance for long. Perhaps no firm emphasis should be laid upon the fact that the manor, when granted to Robert de Ufford in 1332, had been held to be worth as much as £150 (225 marks).[25] What is much more to the point is this: when, on 5 July 1388, Countess Isabel took out a royal pardon for having failed to obtain a licence for having previously leased the manor to Michael for term of her life, it was stated that the annual farm he had agreed to pay her was 200 marks *plus* the rent of £10 due to the queen as dower— 215 marks in all.[26] It would appear that Michael's prospective annual gain when Costessey became his by reversion would hardly be less than £11 18s 3d,[27] not taking into account the general tendency for extents of land, upon which the Exchequer relied for its calculations, to result in under-assessments. The manor must surely have been undervalued in the extent on which the exchange of 3 August 1384 was based. But from the terms of the countess's pardon of 1388 one other significant fact is palpable: Michael, unwilling to wait for the countess's death (upon which the promised reversion depended), had meantime secured actual possession of Costessey. Moreover, he had contrived to do so by means of a lease agreed with the countess privately. Nor, in his eagerness, had he lost much time: the reversion was his on 3 August 1384, and by 1 March 1385 he was not only in possession of the manor but had already settled it, for the countess's lifetime, on a group of feoffees of his own choosing.[28] Admittedly, for this enfeoff-ment he took out on that date a royal licence by letters patent under the great seal; but the lease agreed between him and the countess was without any such authorisation (which, clearly, it had required, hence the countess's own later pardon); and so the transaction was fundamentally improper, quite apart from Michael's having misused his authority as chancellor to sanction the enfeoffment.

Then again, even though Michael had so exploited the royal grant of the reversion of Costessey as to have obtained a private lease of the manor for as long as the grant was in suspense, he was evidently still not satisfied that full advantage had been taken of the king's willingness to convert the payment of 180 marks, which he was continuing to derive from the Hull customs, into income from *other*, alternative sources, once more including landed estate. For on 22 November 1385, not long after his creation as earl (and in addition to all he had recently been given to support his new rank), he secured, in lieu of the 180 marks, an annual grant of £29 from the fee-farm of Winchester, £47 13s 4d from the farm of Rockingham castle and the stewardship of the royal forests between Oxford and Stamford, together with, to the value of £43 6s 8d, the manor of Haslebury Plucknett (Somerset), which manor had been held by the king's half-brother, Thomas Holland, earl of Kent, until the death of their mother (on 8 August 1385) when Holland's entry into his inheritance by reversion had put the manor at the king's disposal.[29] Contained in this grant, not least in the manor of Haslebury Plucknett, which was well able to meet the charge imposed, were sources of assured income far preferable to levies of the 'ancient custom' of 6s 8d per sack on wool exported from Hull.

All these acts of malversation which came under scrutiny from the Commons in 1386—and the fourth and fifth articles of Michael's impeachment increased, of course, the gravamen of the charge—must be seen against the background of other, additional benefits which he had been able to secure during his earlier years in office as chancellor. Those benefits were usually quite profitable, financially as well as in other ways: a grant of a weekly market and annual fair at Messingham (Lincolnshire), on 2 May 1383; a grant of the view of frankpledge and of the assize of bread and ale at Appleby, Risby and Santon (Lincolnshire), on 1 November 1383; a grant of the view of frankpledge at Stratford St Mary and Higham St Mary (Suffolk), of a weekly market and an annual fair, again, at Stratford St Mary, together with rights of free warren there and at Dedham (Essex), on 20 July 1384.[30] He was also given, on 27 April 1385, a royal licence to crenellate his Suffolk manor houses at Wingfield, Sternfield and Huntingfield, and to enclose parks at the first two of these places and also at Stradbrook.[31] But this series of grants was mainly of incorporeal rights, and they all related to existing family possessions. They were not grants of lands, still less of new ones. So Michael's statement, made when he first answered this first charge brought against him—that save by means of the exchange of the 400 marks annuity he had received no lands from the king until made an earl—appears to be correct. That exchange, however, had been a measure by which he derived considerable financial advantage. What Michael had managed to do, by a short series of basically three royal grants spread over three and a half years (the grants of 23 May 1382, 3 August 1384 and 22 November 1385), the last two obtained while he was chancellor, was to have converted an annuity of 400 marks charged on the Hull customs, a source of income unsatisfactory because found difficult to retain, and in any case not dependable, into revenue mainly derived from landed estate: the manors involved were annually worth 255 marks, that is, nearly two-thirds of the annuity. The likelihood is, however, that the extents had been in Michael's favour and the manors underassessed, and that what he gained as a result of his exchange of the annuity was an increase of assured revenue over insecure revenue, an increase of the order of either twenty-odd or thirty-odd per cent of the nominal value. It is very doubtful, therefore, whether the exchange was as 'true' as Michael had alleged when first answering the charge. And, so far as Benhall and Dedham are concerned, Michael's willingness to pay 1,000 marks for the bondsmen and woodlands of these manors suggests that he was aware that, in the existing extents forming the basis of calculation when the exchange was negotiated, they had been undervalued. Under the terms of the judgment of the 1386 parliament, he was to forfeit both manors. When precisely they were lost to him cannot be said: not until 24 February 1388 was Dedham leased out by the Exchequer;[32] nor until 5 June following, Benhall.[33]

Regarding the Commons' insinuation that Michael's promotion as earl of Suffolk was undeserved, his own defence was, so far as the record goes, modest and expressed in general terms. He disclaimed any unworthy personal ambition; insisted that it was by the king's command that he had assumed his new rank, and that on the same occasion, moreover, others had been raised to even higher dignities (*sc.* Edmund of Langley and

Thomas of Woodstock, Richard's uncles, to dukedoms);
alluded to his military and diplomatic services, in the
performance of which he had suffered misfortune and financial
loss; and said that his elevation had been formally confirmed in
parliament, where all the necessary ceremonies had been
publicly performed. It was something to Michael's credit that
Richard, lord Scrope of Bolton, was ready to speak for him,
and most probably to his benefit that he did so. Admittedly,
Scrope had been husband to Michael's now deceased sister
Blanche (*ob.* 1379), and the two men, as members of John of
Gaunt's retinue both at home and abroad, had also been
companions-in-arms. But Scrope's administrative record and
personal reputation entitled his testimony to great respect: he
had been treasurer of the Exchequer, March 1371–September
1375; under Richard II he had been steward of the royal
Household, August 1377–October 1378; he had only relinquished that position in order that he might take custody of the
great seal, which he retained until January 1380, and he had
again been chancellor from December 1381 until July 1382,
being then, after a prudent administration, unjustifiably
dismissed for (according to Thomas Walsingham) his com-
mendably vigorous resistance to the king's excessive liberality
to favourites.[34] When vindicating Michael's worthiness for
promotion to an earldom, Scrope evidently directed attention
to such of his merits as might carry most weight with their
parliamentary peers: his long career as a knight and his
multifarious services to the Crown. He apparently made no
allusion to Michael's social origins, and this silence may well
have been thought eloquent by some.[35] But what Scrope did
mention was that Michael's career had witnessed no rapid
transition from lowly estate to his present position; moreover,
in saying that Michael had owned property well able to support
his previous baronial rank he was only telling the truth.
Michael's own lands—the family lands in Yorkshire (more
particularly in the East Riding), in the parts of Lindsey in
Lincolnshire, and in Durham, augmented by the estates in East
Anglia deriving from his marriage with the heiress of the

Wingfields—were in fact very extensive and valuable, amply sufficient to sustain a career which, as the brief record of Scrope's testimony implies, had been of some distinction even before Michael had become chancellor and, until then, certainly respectable enough.

Born *c.* 1330, Michael had spent his youth in what, for his family as a whole, was an atmosphere of great emotional strain. This was a direct result of the ambitious involvement of his father, William de la Pole, as leader of the country's wool merchants and the most important native English banker of the period, in Edward III's ingenious but risky schemes for financing his war against France.[36] Certainly, William had his ups-and-downs. As a victim of the king's anger at the miscarriage of his plans, he was imprisoned from November 1340 until May 1342. In 1343, however, he had made a come-back as founder of the syndicate which then first took over the farming of the customs; and it also fell to him to organise the methods which were used to finance the successful campaigns of 1345–7, and which remained in force until 1349. Even so, he was to face the possibility of personal ruin once more, in 1354. Then, he was again imprisoned on fresh charges of peculation and fraud, and Edward III finally threatened to have William's trial of 1341, formally annulled in 1344, reopened. It was only some three months after William's capitulation in face of this renewal of royal hostility, the capitulation represented by the settlement of 30 November 1354 (see p. 119), that on 4 March 1355 Michael became his father's attorney-general in the courts.[37] To what extent, if at all, Michael then or later salvaged for himself what remained of his father's mercantile and financial 'empire' is not known. However, his family origin (and, most probably, William's unsavoury reputation too) was always to be held against him by his detractors. Thomas Walsingham of St Albans was more than once to harp upon it, referring to him in socially disparaging as well as politically hostile terms: 'qui fuerat a pueritia magis mercimoniis, utpote mercator, mercatoris filius, quam militia, occupatus'; 'vir plus aptus mercimoniis quam militiae, et qui trapezetis in pace consenuerat, non armatis in bello'.[38]

Such a disdainful testimony as Walsingham's will stand up against neither Lord Scrope's recorded observations on Michael's behalf during the trial of 1386, nor the known facts of Michael's career, which bear out that report. It was in 1355, the year following the last crisis in William de la Pole's affairs, and a year which roughly fits Scrope's estimate in 1386 of the beginning of Michael's career in arms ('avoit travaillé a Baner par xxx ans et plus'), that Michael first undertook military service, only for the intended expedition (which was to have assisted Edward III's ally, Charles of Navarre, in Normandy) to prove abortive. Michael had joined the force as a member of the retinue of Henry of Grosmont,[39] first duke of Lancaster, one of the most renowned of Edward's captains-of-war and a founder-member of the Order of the Garter. It was as one of the Black Prince's company that, in October 1359, he joined the great army which, led by the king, waged the disappointing campaign that ended with the treaty of Brétigny (May 1360).[40] First summoned to parliament as a knight banneret in January 1366,[41] Michael again crossed the Channel in 1369 when, the French having renounced that treaty, war was resumed; this time he went out in the retinue of John of Gaunt,[42] who made raids in the march of Calais and into Picardy in August and September but, after an unsuccessful siege of Harfleur, came home in November. This was quite possibly one of the two occasions on which he was said to have been a prisoner-of-war.[43] It was probably again in Lancaster's retinue that in 1370 Michael served in Aquitaine, taking part in September in the siege of Limoges; and certainly, after the Black Prince's return home, he assisted John of Gaunt at the siege of Montpont sur l'Isle (in Périgord), which place fell in February 1371.[44] Presumably coming back to England with Lancaster in the following November, he was among the ducal retinue which in August 1372 was to have joined Edward III's force going to the relief of Thouars, but which never left the English coast. From Calais a year later (August 1373) he accompanied the *chivauchée* which Lancaster led through the heart of France to Bordeaux,[45] where, only shortly before Christmas, the army arrived utterly exhausted and, although it had failed to provoke any major encounter with the enemy, much reduced in numbers. (Michael was still in Gascony in March 1374 when Pope Gregory XI requested his good offices on behalf of papal nuncios who were about to interview the duke.)[46] He now seems to have been well established as a Lancastrian retainer; and although his connexions with Hull[47] may have had some bearing on his promotion as admiral of the king's fleet north of the Thames on 24 November 1376, this appointment must have more directly depended upon his friendship with John of Gaunt who, Edward III being now old and incapable, was then virtually head of the government. Reappointed admiral under Richard II (on 14 August 1377), Michael retained the office then, however, only briefly (until 5 December following).[48] Appointed in April 1378 as a commissioner to take over the castle of Brest when Duke John IV of Brittany put this base at the disposal of his English allies, he also participated in Lancaster's useless expedition against Saint-Malo in the following summer. This was Michael's last military employment, save for Richard II's inglorious incursion into Scotland of 1385 which, as chancellor, he accompanied, and with a large retinue of sixty men-at-arms and eighty archers. Military service, then, Michael had rendered in plenty, and if this was on expeditions and campaigns which had never yielded any great advantage, and were sometimes even fiascos, that was nothing to his personal discredit. Precisely on what occasions he had been taken prisoner-of-war is not known. There is, however, no reason to doubt his statement at his trial that this misfortune, one liable to be very expensive as giving rise to payment of ransom, had befallen him twice. In the company then present, to err on such a point would have been fatuous.

One such occasion of imprisonment abroad was when, as Michael himself explained, he had been on an embassy arranging for Richard II's marriage; and the circumstances of that incident are something less obscure. On 18 March 1379 he had been commissioned to treat for a marriage with Katherine, daughter of Bernabo Visconti of Milan, and then to go on to Rome for discussions with Pope Urban VI.[49] The Roman Curia, in view of rivalry with Avignon, was only too anxious to procure an alliance between its two principal protagonists, Richard II and Wenzel IV, then newly elected king of the Romans; and Michael was persuaded to open, when returning home through Germany, negotiations for a marriage between Richard and Wenzel's sister Anne (the marriage which, after further exchanges in 1380 and 1381, took place in January 1382).[50] Michael had left London on 26 March 1379, and it was probably in the early autumn that he left Rome. In Germany, his business there concluded, he and his fellow envoys, Sir John de Burley and Sir Gerard de l'Isle (his own son-in-law), had the misfortune to be waylaid and captured, possibly by brigands. This was sometime before 14 December, when a royal herald (Richard Hereford) set out to negotiate for their liberation.[51] It was John of Gaunt, however, who on 19 January 1380 undertook to furnish, in Dordrecht at Easter, a ransom of 7,000 florins (approximately £1,000) to Albert, duke of Bavaria (who may only have been acting as intermediary), on condition that the prisoners were released at the beginning of either February or March.[52] It was not until 20 May following that Michael returned to England. At first no account was taken of his reimbursement for the ransom. However, on 3 June the Exchequer was ordered to pay him his wages and expenses (at the rate of the £2 a day normally allowed a knight banneret on diplomatic service) for the whole period of his absence abroad, including, as a special concession, the time he had spent in imprisonment. As Michael had been paid £400 before leaving England, the Exchequer was now told to pay him an additional £442 (plus £10 10s for the sea passages), the sum still outstanding on that basis.[53] Later, however, but not until 9 January 1384—by which time Michael was chancellor—he was recompensed for his losses on the 1379–80 mission, including the costs of his ransom, to the tune of £933 6s 8d.[54] Even so, this payment was by Exchequer assignment, not with cash in hand;

and it is therefore not improbable that his protestation at his trial, that he had incurred serious financial loss on account of that embassy, was well founded.

In Lord Scrope's apology as recorded, nothing is said of Michael's appointment, late in 1381, to act along with the earl of Arundel as the young king's personal counsellor and governor, the result of a decision, taken in parliament,[55] which, since it was reported to the Commons, must have originated in the Lords and met with their approval. Certainly, however, the length of Michael's chancellorship was mentioned by Scrope as something to his credit. Since his appointment on 13 March 1383, save for two breaks in 1386, one of seven weeks (9 February–28 March), when he was involved in an embassy to France, and the other of three weeks (23 April–14 May), when he had the king's leave to visit Hull on private business,[56] Michael had been in continuous possession of the great seal until his impeachment. Except for Sir John Knyvet, who had held office for all but the last six months of Edward III's last five years, no layman had ever been chancellor for so long. (Scrope's own two periods of office, under Richard II, had even together fallen short of two years.) The chancellorship, an office of great responsibility, was very rewarding financially, quite apart from the opportunities it offered of legitimate benefits "on the side". Over and above the customary fees and wages attached to the office *ab antiquo*, Michael (like Scrope before him) enjoyed a *regardum* of 400 marks a year in aid of official costs and expenses which, for the whole of his chancellorship of roughly three and a half years, amounted to £963. And, although by the time of his dismissal nearly half of this sum (£472-odd) was still in arrears, he had been fortunate enough to receive early in his tenure (30 July 1383) as much as £346, more by nearly a third than what was due to him for the whole of his first twelve months in office.[57]

Of course, exploitation and misuse of office such as was now in 1386 being attributed to Michael could only weaken the intended force of Scrope's reference to length of tenure of office—indeed, make that duration something of an aggravation in itself. That there had developed some dissatisfaction on this very point is suggested in one of the articles preferred at the trial, during the 'Merciless Parliament' of 1388, of Sir Simon de Burley, the king's under-chamberlain, and his associates.[58] These courtiers were then charged with having aided Richard in retaining Michael so long in office in order to promote their treasonable designs, with the result, so it was alleged, that the kingdom had been endangered by the 'malveis governail' characterising that period. Those who opposed a policy of peace with France, which, intended to assist the duke of Lancaster's ambitions in Spain, Michael had advocated, as well as those who, on more general grounds, disliked the development of a 'court party', must have become increasingly suspicious of Michael's rôle in government. And the narrative of Thomas Walsingham of St Albans furnishes ample illustration of the chancellor's growing unpopularity on both counts.[59] Not only was Michael, in the first parliament it fell to him to open as chancellor (October 1383), personally responsible for the impeachment of Bishop Despenser of Norwich, the leader of the recent Flemish crusade, and at that time Lancaster's hated competitor for government funds devoted to military purposes; but also, according to Walsingham, as late as 1385 he still opposed the restitution of Despenser's temporalities, contrary to the advice of Bishop Arundel of Ely. Walsingham also taxed him with showing, in the summer of 1386, unnecessary sympathy to the merchants of the Genoese convoy which, making through the Dover straits towards Flanders, was forced to surrender by a royal fleet guarding the coast, the chancellor having subsequently ordered the restitution of all their cargoes or, if this was not possible, payment of compensation.[60] Regarding this incident, Walsingham says nothing of any bribery. Henry Knighton of Leicester abbey, another hostile witness (despite his Lancastrian affiliations), goes so far, however, as to say that Michael was prompted by receipt of a great bribe to act on his own initiative in this matter and, moreover, that he was impeached of this by the Commons in 1386 ('Et de illo in proximo parliamento accusatus fuit per

Communes').[61] The articles of Michael's impeachment do not mention this. But it is quite possible that this incident was made the basis of a subsidiary charge which, however, was soon dropped.

Considering Michael's growing unpopularity as chancellor, it is remarkable that no extant chronicle of the period refers to the private complaint of his conduct that was lodged in parliament so early in his period of office as 24 May 1384. That complaint is reported in great detail, however, in the parliament-roll.[62] (Since Michael was exonerated, this was no doubt by his arrangement.) A London fishmonger, John Cavendish, who, for lack of adequate naval protection, had lost merchandise by enemy action at sea, had petitioned in the previous parliament (October–November 1383) for compensation from those responsible, only to have his bill referred to the Chancery. He now (in the parliament of April–May 1384) complained that he had been unable to obtain redress there, despite acceptance by the chancellor's clerk of a bribe in kind (fish for the chancellor, cloth for the clerk) in return for which he was to have the chancellor's 'good lordship and aid' in his suit. Cavendish admitted, however, that the chancellor might originally have been unaware of what his clerk had been up to, and that in any case he had subsequently been paid for the fish, leaving it to the Lords to decide whether this had been done 'pur loialte et conscience' or to evade 'esclandre et reproche en le cas'. Michael had no difficulty in clearing himself: only legal difficulties, not intentional dilatoriness on his own part, he said, had prevented an expeditious settlement of the action (as royal judges and serjeants-at-law could vouch); moreover, he went on, as soon as he had discovered that the present of fish was a bribe, being greatly distressed and angry, on an oath taken in the suitor's presence he had disclaimed all knowledge of his clerk's transaction, caused the offending covenant to be cancelled, and paid for the fish. The Lords accepted this explanation and granted Michael's request that Cavendish should be arrested and only allowed bail pending judgment regarding the slander committed in parliament. A commission of judges and officials later investigated this point and awarded Michael damages of 1,000 marks, the culprit to be imprisoned until that sum (plus a fine to the Crown) had been paid. Not until 6 October 1384 was the order given for Cavendish's release from Windsor Castle, and later (28 February 1385) he entered into a bond to be of good behaviour towards the chancellor.[63] That such charges could be levelled against the chancellor at all suggests hostility towards his commercial policy on the part of the London victuallers, of whom, as a fishmonger, Cavendish was one. It certainly reflects Michael's early unpopularity in certain quarters. Parliament, however, was still far from dissatisfied at that stage of his chancellorship. The attack had broken down. But perhaps some of the mud stuck.

Whatever general discontents Michael's administration as chancellor had aroused by the time he was made earl of Suffolk, there can be no doubt that that promotion aggravated the dislike in which, outside court circles, he was held, and was in itself a source of grievance. For him to say, as he did at his trial, that he had not himself urged his advancement, that it was all of the king's own doing, and that parliament had confirmed it, was neither here nor there. There was evidence enough of personal ambition in his mere acceptance of the honour. It gave entry into the ranks of the earls who now numbered eleven out of sixty-two lay peers in all. His choice of Suffolk for his title was not inappropriate, if only because he held (*jure uxoris*) considerable estates in the county and was already possessed by royal grant of some of the escheated lands of William de Ufford, his predecessor in the title.[64] Otherwise, it may perhaps be considered to have been unfortunate, as drawing attention to the contrast between his own and his family's reputations and those of the late earl's. William de Ufford, second earl of the name, who had married a great-granddaughter of Edward I for his first wife, and had followed both his father and a brother into membership of the Order of the Garter, had been held (so Walsingham tells us)[65] in universal esteem, and was mourned at his death by all ranks in society. Nor was it ever really helpful to Michael that his promotion during Richard II's expedition to

Scotland, by a charter attested by magnates including the duke of Lancaster and seven earls, had been simultaneously accompanied by other promotions, the elevation of the king's younger uncles, Edmund, earl of Cambridge, and Thomas, earl of Buckingham, to the dukedoms of York and Gloucester, respectively.[66] Titles of great dignity were, of course, something in themselves. Their conferment had greater meaning and value, however, when accompanied by royal grants to the recipients, especially if such grants proved effectual. And the ill-feeling provided by the elevation to comital rank of a merchant's son—what among at least some of the titular nobility must have been regarded as a disgraceful affront to the rank—was, in a period of royal financial stress, certainly increased by the emoluments Michael received from the king, ostensibly to sustain his new dignity. We must now turn to the question of those emoluments, their nature and value.

In accordance with the charter of Michael's creation as earl, dated at Hoselaw (in Teviotdale, Scotland) on 6 August 1385,[67] he and his successors in the title, the heirs-male of his body, were to receive £20 a year from the farm of the county of Suffolk, at the hands of the sheriff. Then, under the terms of a supplemental charter, dated at Newcastle upon Tyne on 20 August,[68] he was granted, also in tail male, the reversion of lands which had escheated on the death of the late earl, to the value of £500 a year. Perhaps Michael was correct in saying at his trial that it had been intended he should have as much land as his predecessors in the title; if so, that intention was unfulfilled, for the lands the Uffords had originally been granted were to have been worth 1,000 marks (£666 13s 4d). Certainly, however, he was entirely right in saying that at the time of his promotion the Ufford lands allocated for his endowment were not, in fact, available, being held for life by Queen Anne and William de Ufford's widow.[69] Hence the grant only in reversion. So far as those lands were concerned, Michael could only be given a promise of them, a promise dependent for its fulfilment upon the deaths of the queen and the dowager countess when his grant in reversion could apply.[70] Obviously, some alternative scheme was needed to provide for the endowment, and this was what the Newcastle charter went on to supply: until the Ufford lands did become available, he was to have, instead, £200 a year from the issues of the Hanaper of the Chancery, together with lands and revenues making up the remaining £300. These estates and rents, previously held by the king's half-brother, Thomas Holland, earl of Kent, had recently been liberated for fresh disposal by the Crown when Thomas inherited lands from his mother (Joan of Kent), following her death on 8 August 1385 (only two days after Michael's promotion to his earldom).[71] What comprised these lands and rents were the manor of Lowestoft with the hundred of Lothingland (Suffolk) and the manor of Wendover (Buckinghamshire), valued respectively at £66 13s 4d and £74 13s 4d a year, and annual payments of £100 from the issues of the castle and town of Marlborough (Wiltshire), £31 from the fee-farm normally rendered at the Exchequer by the prior of Barnwell for the town of Chesterton (Cambridgeshire), and £37 13s 4d from the fee-farm of the city of Winchester. The sum of this estimated annual income came not to £300, but to £310. The extra £10, however, was additionally conceded with the intention that it should offset a rent of just that amount which Michael was under obligation to pay the queen, as a charge on the manor of Costessey (Norfolk), which manor, granted as dower to William de Ufford's widow in 1382, had been leased by the latter to Michael (see above, p. 122), probably early in 1385, certainly previous to his promotion as earl. And so a balance was struck. Incidentally, it was also provided that this £10 rent should lapse on the queen's death, and that another rent from Costessey, one of £1 8s 5d payable to the Crown, for which Michael, instead of the countess, had become liable as her lessee in the manor, should cease, too, when *she* died. Moreover, when Michael's lease of Costessey ended and (under the terms of his grant of the reversion) he became owner of the manor, payment to the king of yet another rent with which the manor was encumbered, again one of £10, was to stop whenever peace should be made with France. (This rent was owing to the

Crown in the meantime because, being normally due to the abbey of Bonrepos in Brittany, it had been sequestrated for the duration of the French war.) It was an automatic condition of the charter of 20 August as a whole, that whenever parcels of the Ufford lands reverted to the Crown and then, of course, passed to Michael (as would happen at the death of either the queen or the countess), equivalent deductions were to be made from the income alternatively provided by the charter.

The supplementary Newcastle charter of 20 August 1385[72] was re-formed in letters patent issued under the great seal at Westminster on 8 September,[73] only for this grant to be followed directly, on 12 September, by yet another royal patent.[74] The intention of this last grant was to clarify Michael and his male heirs' future possession of the Ufford lands, or rather to specify the estates in question. (The key words of this patent of 12 September were 'in speciali nominavimus et assignavimus'.) What was eventually to revert was even now defined, the extents made when the queen and the dowager countess had taken possession being used as the basis of assessment. Of the queen's present holdings Michael was promised the castle, town, manor and honour of Eye to the value of £173 6s 8d a year (the full annual value of £200 reduced to take account of the rent of forty marks Michael already owed the honour for his own nearby, dependent manor of Strad-brook), the hundred of Hartismere and Stow to the annual value of £16, and a yearly farm rent of £23 16s 8d from the manor of Combs (near Stowmarket), all in Suffolk; up in Norfolk, about ten miles roughly north of Norwich, the neighbouring manors of Cawston and Burgh-by-Aylesham to the value of £53 6s 8d and £31 8s 10¼d a year, respectively; and in Essex, the manor of Gestingthorpe to the value of £12 a year. Of the countess's dower lands, he was promised two other Suffolk manors, those of Haughley (close to Stowmarket) and Thorndon (near Eye), valued at £97 10s 11d and £35 13s 7¾d a year, respectively. The queen's death would bring Michael and his heirs Ufford lands and revenues from land worth £309 18s 10¼d, and the countess's death, lands worth £133 4s 6¾d; the two portions combined would make up a value of £443 3s 5d per annum. This was still short of the original endowment of £500 a year: another £56 16s 7d was needed. And so, to make up that total, Michael was to be allowed to retain the manor of Lowestoft and the hundred of Lothingland, which he would have himself been holding all along as a part of the alternative arrangement provided for in the charter of 20 August (and by the letters patent of 8 September) 1385. The annual income from this item, estimated at £66 13s 4d (100 marks), exceeded what was required by £9 16s 9d, a small difference which Michael was to pay the Crown as a rent.

What was meant by this series of grants (not counting the £20 annuity from the county farm of Suffolk or the incidental concessions arising from Michael's occupation of Costessey as lessee) was that pending the reversion of the Ufford lands after possibly a long, and certainly an indefinite, period of waiting, he received (under the charter of 20 August and by the letters patent of 8 September 1385) nearly three-tenths[75] of the value of his endowment of £500 a year in landed estate, roughly a third from other sources of assured royal revenue,[76] and the rest, precisely two-fifths, from the Hanaper of the Chancery, which was bound to be another reliable source as long as he remained chancellor; and that, lest there should be any question of the identity or financial adequacy of the Ufford lands he was eventually to secure permanently, these lands were, within a matter of days of the original grant (i.e. on 12 September 1385), all defined as reversionary. Such an anticipatory specification was quite unusual. Furthermore, so generously was Michael provided for in this 'assignment' that when it was realised that the Ufford lands allocated would fall short of his total endowment (£500 a year), the deficit was made good by a permission to retain lands and rights, namely, a portion of the originally alternative provision (viz. the manor of Lowestoft and the hundred of Lothingland). The value of these latter was actually in excess of what was required, and so Michael and his successors in the title were being left in the prospectively happy position of needing to make a repayment, if only a marginal repayment, to the Crown. Besides, not only were all save one of the Ufford estates situated in East Anglia (indeed, within very easy reach of many of Michael's own manors there), but were generally of high individual value, few in number therefore, and so comparatively easy and economical to manage administratively.

The charge against Michael was partly that he had not deserved such a large endowment when promoted to his earldom, and that, in accepting it, he was contravening the oath he had taken as chancellor to prevent loss to the Crown. His defence (it will be recalled) was: that grants made to others, promoted at the same time, had not been impugned; that as chancellor he was free to seal any grants sanctioned by the king; and that his own grants had been so approved, the king having been made fully aware beforehand of the financial consequences. The charge was partly, too, that the value of what he was then granted had been underestimated, with the implication that he had received as endowment more than he was strictly entitled to. The grant alluded to in this part of the charge was, it seems clear, the grant of those Ufford lands which, conceded in reversion by the Newcastle charter of 20 August 1385, were specified in the letters patent of 12 September, together with their annual values, and *not* the temporary, alternative grant made by that charter and confirmed in the letters patent of 8 September. In fact, this alternative provision was obviously not, in the main, a grant of lands, but a grant of royal revenues and rents from various sources, sources which included lands but did so only partially: such lands as were included—the manor of Lowestoft (with the hundred of Lothingland) and the manor of Wendover—were together worth no more than £141 6s 8d out of the £500 granted, a fraction of nearer a quarter than a third of the total. Admittedly, it is almost certain that these manors were worth more than as assessed: Lowestoft was to be valued in 1389[77] at £70 a year (as against £66 13s 4d in Michael's grant), and Wendover in 1388[78] at £84 a year (as against £74 13s 4d), jointly an increase of £12 13s 4d (one of roughly nine per cent). But if that was all, the undervaluation was nothing very considerable; and, in any event, the extents used in Michael's case were both as used at the time of the grant of the manors, in March 1380, to the king's half-brother, Thomas Holland, earl of Kent.[79] But, then, the question of undervaluation relates mainly to the Ufford lands Michael was intended to enjoy only eventually.

When, in the Newcastle charter of 20 August 1385, Michael was promised Ufford lands to the value of £500 a year, possession of which was to be contingent upon the deaths of the present holders, namely, the queen and the dowager countess, it was deemed only reasonable that what he would then obtain under the reversion should be determined on the basis of valuations made subsequent to those events; and this was in fact what the charter stated ('juxta extentam bonam et racionabilem inde post decessum Regine et Isabelle comitesse Suffolkie . . . *faciendam*').[80] When, however, very soon afterwards—indeed, forthwith (on 12 September 1385)—it was decided actually to specify in advance those Ufford lands which Michael should enjoy, it was obviously necessary—because to implement this decision required an immediate calculation—to decide also whether fresh *ad hoc* valuations of the estates so named should be made, or whether recourse should be had to the most recent existing extents, viz. those upon which had been based the queen's and the countess's grants of 1382. The latter course was the one adopted ('juxta extentam inde . . . prefatis Regine et comitisse *factam*').[81] But what was the point of actually specifying, so far in advance of real need, the estates Michael was only to obtain at indefinite, and haply long-deferred, future dates? Why all the rush? Might it be that the extents made in 1382 were believed, or were now known, to have resulted in undervaluations? And if so, was the decision that Michael should be granted the letters patent of 12 September 1385, containing the 'nominations and assignments' of Ufford lands of which he had so recently been given the reversion, a decision taken in the light of that belief or knowledge? That grant of 12 September, with all its specifications, obviously embodied a change of plan of sorts. Was this change of plan decided upon only with a view to investing Michael's grant of 20 August with a greater validity? Or was it decided upon simply in order to use those extents of 1382, the facts of which were known, in preference to risking fresh extents from which higher valuations might possibly result? (Higher valuations would mean either a reduction in the lands promised, or rents being reserved to the Crown in order not to exceed the total value granted.) It is difficult to avoid the conclusion that the change of plan, as represented by the grant of 12 September, was designed to enable recourse to be had to the extents of 1382. Of course, in defending himself against the charge that the lands were undervalued, and that he therefore received a larger grant than might otherwise have been the case, Michael contended that the decision behind the grant of 12 September had been taken only after some dispute, or at least discussion, in which his own conduct, so he alleged, had been entirely correct. He himself, he said, had suggested fresh extents; and he declared that it was only after the king had objected that if lower, more favourable assessments resulted from new enquiries made while he was chancellor, the validity of those assessments might be challenged, that he accepted the extents already available, the extents, that is, of 1382. These, Michael insisted, had not only been made before he was chancellor, but were greatly to the king's advantage, being 'the highest valuations' (as he put it). But was this latter assertion true?

In presenting such evidence as has been discovered bearing upon this question, certain considerations must needs always be borne in mind. Valuations of the Ufford lands are so sparse as hardly to furnish any proper test or comparison. Moreover, in some instances they derive from reports or references arising out of a long stretch of time: from the early years of Edward III to the end of the century, a period in which, for demographic and other economic reasons, land values in general can only have been subject to considerable fluctuations and, possibly for the most part, affected adversely. In any case, extents were not only notoriously erratic, but also tended to err on the side of undervaluation. All the same, they were what the Exchequer had perforce to make do with, when, for example, pitching the level of farm rents and other such renders to the Crown. But here follows the evidence, such as it is, and for what it is worth, relating to the Ufford lands which, under the terms of the letters patent of 12 September 1385, would eventually revert to Michael.

Three of the most valuable estates, all three in Suffolk, were the castle, town and manor of Eye (extended when granted to the queen in 1382 at £200 per annum), the manor of Haughley (extended when then granted to the countess at £97 10s 11d), and the manor of Thorndon (extended when similarly granted at £35 13s 7¾d), all these extents being used again in 1385. The combined annual value of these estates as then estimated—£333 4s 6¾d—was all but exactly two-thirds of what Michael had been granted in reversion (£500). Only in the case of Haughley, however, is there evidence to make possible a simple, direct comparison of assessments: in 1339, when granted to Robert de Ufford, Haughley had been reckoned as worth £126 5s 7½d a year.[82] The reduction in value between 1339 and 1382 being as much as £28 14s 8½d (a drop of about twenty-three per cent), either the manor had greatly declined or the extent on the later occasion had produced a considerable underestimate. A comparison of assessments of the value of each of the other two properties, Eye and Thorndon, is possible only if combined with Haughley or when the two are taken together. Eye and Haughley, the sum of whose values in 1382 was £297 10s 11d, had been jointly farmed by the Crown in 1330 at an annual rent of £373 6s 8d,[83] representing a *reduction* in assessed value, by 1382, of some £75 (a drop of about twenty per cent). Eye and Thorndon, however, the sum of whose values in 1382 was £235 13s 7¾d, had been jointly assessed in 1337, when settled on Robert de Ufford, at no more than £207 1s 0½d,[84] representing an *increase* in assessed value, by 1382, of £28 12s 7¼d (a rise of about fourteen per cent).[85] Passing on to the evidence linking Haughley and Thorndon, we find that whereas in 1382 the sum of their annual values was £133 4s 6¾d, in 1398 Michael's son and heir was to be granted, pending the reversion of the two manors, a yearly recompense of £123 7s 9¾d,[86] which means that, if this was a really equivalent sum, their jointly computed income was nearly £10 higher in 1382 than in 1398. Either the two manors had declined in value since 1382 or the then extents, taken together, had not involved underassessment.

The estate assigned to Michael on 12 September 1385 first in importance among those Ufford lands not already mentioned above, was the manor of Cawston (Norfolk). In the early years of Edward III (whence comes, unfortunately, the only evidence of its value available for comparison), Cawston had been quite consistently reckoned to be worth £60 a year.[87] Its annual value when assigned to the queen in 1382 had been set at £53 6s 8d (a drop of about eleven per cent). Underassessment, in first the queen's favour and then, of course, in Michael's, is not impossible in this instance. Such a charge, however, is much more likely to have been true regarding the manor of Burgh-by-Aylesham (Norfolk), another estate in the queen's portion of the Ufford lands. For although, having been valued in 1327 at £30,[88] its annual worth was put in 1382 at £31 8s 10¼d, the queen had been able, as recently as February 1385, to lease it for life at a yearly rent of £36;[89] and if the lessee was to derive a profit, clearly it was worth even more. Regarding the possibility of an underassessment of the value of the hundred of Hartismere and Stow (Suffolk), another of the queen's sources of income which was to revert to Michael at her death, all that can be said is that when grants of the hundred had been made in 1330 (to Edward II's mother)[90] and in 1337 (to Robert de Ufford)[91] its annual value had been taken to be £20, whereas the extent of 1382 (and Michael's 'assignment' of 1385) measured its worth at only £16 a year. Of the manor of Gestingthorpe (Essex), another Ufford manor 'assigned' to Michael in 1385 which, when granted to the queen in 1382, had been extended at £12 a year, no more can be said than that in 1349 only a third of it had been valued at half that figure (£6).[92] Concerning the manor of Combs (Suffolk), no question of a charge of under-assessment could possibly arise: what here the queen held (and Michael was 'assigned') was simply the long-established annual fee-farm rent of £23 16s 8d.[93]

Regarding this question of the charge of underassessment in 1382 and, consequently, in 1385 as well, the extreme difficulty of coming to any safe conclusion will be readily allowed. In some instances, e.g. Eye—the largest single source of contributory revenue—the evidence available for comparison from the early years of Edward III's reign is virtually unusable, being ambiguous or even contradictory. The evidence for the rest, taken at its face value, suggests, however, that in 1382 (and 1385) lower assessments than heretofore were generally the case. Even so, if such underassessments were in fact made, these did not represent, in absolute monetary terms, very considerable gains for either the queen or the dowager countess, or (prospectively) Michael. Moreover, the fact that the joint value of two important manors—Haughley and Thorndon—was assessed at a higher figure in 1382 than in 1398 (not all that long afterwards) must necessarily pose this question: may not the assessments of 1382 (used in 1385), even if lower than previous ones, have been realistic and fair, indeed 'the highest valuations' possible at the time of their making? No firm conclusion is really attainable; the question remains open. And, in any case, was not the king's insistence, at the time of Michael's promotion, that the extents of 1382, *not* fresh ones, should be the basis of the grants, a sufficient answer in relation to this aspect of the charge? Moreover, if the valuations of 1382 were used, no one could attribute their inadequacy or unfairness to positive official interference on Michael's part (he not being chancellor at that time); and, if those valuations did indeed represent underassessments, Michael was not the only one to benefit. The queen and the countess of Suffolk, whose endowments rested on the same basis, had already benefited, and would presumably continue to do so until they died. If Michael had offended, so, from now on, would they too be offending.

Regarding Michael's endowment in aid of his comital status, what is *known* to have been resented in 1386 was that use had been made of existing extents of such Ufford lands as were promised him when available, those assessments being deemed by the prosecution to have been underassessments (with the result that Michael had in prospect the enjoyment of a larger endowment than would otherwise have been the case). There is no explicit evidence to indicate that resentment was felt that the grant in reversion of 12 September 1385, specifically establishing what Michael's future holdings of Ufford lands were to be, should have been hurried through, not merely while he was still chancellor, but even within little more than a month of his promotion to the earldom. Nor is there evidence that objection had been initially taken to the form of his endowment. It is, however, possible—certainly, it is conceivable—that here lay one of the chief causes of adverse criticism. Obviously, Michael was thought to have done too well. Were there any men thought not to have done well enough, or even not well at all, and were such men themselves acutely conscious of the fact, and very seriously disgruntled as a result? In this connexion, it would at least seem worthwhile to examine the fortunes of those two important members of the royal family proper who had been promoted to dukedoms at the same time as Michael was made earl: Richard II's uncles, Edmund of Langley and Thomas of Woodstock, who had been made duke of York and duke of Gloucester, respectively. Had these two great nobles grounds for dissatisfaction, not to say umbrage?

To take, first, Edmund of Langley, earl of Cambridge since 1362, and aged forty-four in 1385. He had, of course, been endowed by Edward III with considerable estates—by 1348 the lands north of Trent once held by John de Warenne (late earl of Surrey), since 1363 the manors of Stamford and Grantham, and since 1373 the lordship of Wark in Tynedale. But all along under Richard II he had been disappointed of other lands which he had been led to expect, following grants made to him during his father's last year.[94] Admittedly, early in Richard's reign (20 November 1377) he had been confirmed in possession of Fotheringay and other lands[95] given him in tail male on 25 May 1377.[96] But these estates yielded only half the income of an annuity of 1,000 marks allowed him in the previous autumn (3 November 1376); and the remainder (500 marks) was left payable by the Exchequer until such time as more lands became available.[97] Evidently none did; and Edmund's difficulties in obtaining that annual sum from the Exchequer were such that, in February 1380, he had to make do, for the time being, with the farm for the wardship of Thomas, lord Despenser.[98] And, as regards the promised entailment, so the matter still rested when, on 6 August 1385, Edmund was created duke of York, and was promised, as a grant to him and his heirs male in support of the title, an *additional* landed income of £1,000 a year, this sum to be paid in the meantime by the Exchequer.[99] The immediate outcome was again disappointing. Not only had Edmund secured no lands at all under this latter grant by the time parliament met in October 1386, but the income of £1,000 a year he was to have received at the Exchequer instead had failed to materialise, certainly in very large part. £100 of it derived, as was only to be expected, from the issues of the county of York, but the whole of the remainder, in accordance with letters patent of 15 November 1385,[100] had been charged by Exchequer assignment to revenue from the wool customs, viz. £400 from such levies at Hull, the other £500 from the same source in the port of London. Exchequer assignments, and more particularly those on the customs, were notoriously liable to be unproductive (not to say unrealistic). And the London levies are known to have yielded Edmund nothing at all: despite an agreement that his payments should be given an absolute preference, they were in arrears from the time of the grant.[101] In all this, he bears comparison with his brother Thomas, for the latter's recent experiences had been much the same.

From 1374, the year of his betrothal to Eleanor, elder daughter and coheir of Humphrey de Bohun, earl of Hereford, Essex and Northampton (*ob*. 1373), Thomas of Woodstock's endowment had very largely derived from the Bohun estates; and from June 1380, by which time Eleanor had come of age, Thomas retained permanent possession of her purparty (less her mother's dower).[102] His creation as earl of Buckingham in the meantime, on the eve of Richard II's coronation (15 July 1377), had been marked by a grant of £1,000 a year (to him and the heirs of his body), which was to be paid, until lands became available, first at the Exchequer[103] and then, by an alternative arrangement made on 5 July 1379, out of the farms for the sequestrated estates of certain alien priories.[104] Evidently, lands were not made available, and this alternative arrangement was still in force at the time of the parliament of 1386, being in fact then confirmed (on 24 October).[105] Thomas's treatment since his creation as duke of Gloucester on 6 August 1385 had been even less satisfactory. Then granted in tail male another £1,000 a year in support of his new title,[106] he had not yet received any of the promised lands, and the whole annuity had continued to be derived, as initially provided, from Exchequer revenue and again, moreover, mostly by assignment (as in York's case): by a patent of 12 November 1385[107] this £1,000 was all, save £60 from the fee-farm of the city of Gloucester, to come from the 'ancient custom' on wool exported from London (£500), Boston (£140), Hull (200 marks), Lynn (100 marks), Ipswich (£50) and Yarmouth (£50). Admittedly, by a grant of 17 May 1386[108] the castle and honour of Castle Rising (Norfolk), then held by the duke of Brittany, were to pass to Thomas and his heirs male as soon as they came into the king's hands; but, obviously, this grant made no immediate difference. And how inadequate had been the grant upon the 'ancient custom' (London, the most heavily charged port, having contributed nothing) was made clear when, on 24 August following, not only the 'ancient custom' but also the wool subsidy in the same ports as before was assigned for Thomas's payment.[109] This new patent itself explicitly stated that he had been unable to obtain full payment and, moreover, despite the enlargement of the source of revenue, still anticipated difficulties of collection, the patent providing for any lack of funds to be made good in other places (but without specifying where).[110]

It can hardly be doubted that the practical and effective steps taken in August–September 1385 to implement Michael de la Pole's endowment in support of his earldom, notably the specific allocation of the Ufford lands of which he was to enjoy the reversion, i.e. an estate in expectancy, were greatly resented. Royal partiality could hardly have gone further. In the eyes of some, Michael's promotion to an earldom was evidently bad enough. That members of the royal family so closely related to the king as his uncles of York and Gloucester should be promoted to higher dignities than he, and yet, so far as financial endowment was concerned, come off badly, while he came off as well as could be contrived, was worse still. York was by temperament a fainéant. Gloucester was the reverse. His generally virulent opposition to Richard in the parliament of 1386 is easy to understand. And although there is no evidence to suggest that Gloucester inspired Michael's impeachment so far as these aspects of it are concerned, it is not unreasonable to imagine that he lent his heart-felt sympathy to those directly responsible, i.e. the Commons, and used his influence to sustain them in their attack.[111]

Notes

1   *Rot. Parl.*, III, 216a.
2   Ibid., 216b.
3   Ibid., 218a.
4   Ibid., 218b.
5   Ibid., 219a.
6   *CPR, 1354–58*, 158–9.
7   E. B. Fryde, 'The Last Trials of Sir William de la Pole', *Economic History Review*, 2nd ser., XV, 17–30.
8   Ibid., 29. Most of these outstanding debts dated from when William had taken the lead among English wool-exporters in financing the French war in 1337–40.
9   All the charters relating to these manors (*Cal. Charter Rolls, 1327–41*, 446, 470; *CPR, 1338–40*, 383) were surrendered on 7 March 1355 (*CCR, 1354–60*, 195).
10 *Cal. Inqs. p.m., Edward III*, XII, 55.
11 *CCR, 1377–81*, 25.
12 *Rot. Parl.*, III, 127b.
13 *CPR, 1381–85*, 122–3; the grant Michael surrendered was assigned on the following day to Queen Anne as part of her dower (ibid., 126).
14 Subsequently, on 7 August 1382, Michael was, by a separate

grant, conceded Benhall and Dedham with all feudal rights, and with all the franchises William de Ufford had enjoyed (*CPR, 1381–85*, 156).

15 *CPR, 1334–38*, 418; ibid., *1338–40*, 265; *CCR, 1339–41*, 498; ibid., *1343–46*, 437; ibid., *1349–54*, 118.

16 *CPR, 1334–37*, 479.

17 *CFR, 1383–91*, 211; *CPR, 1388–92*, 126.

18 200 m—120 m (Benhall) *minus* 10 m (Dedham).

19 200 m—120 m (Benhall) *plus* £28 10s 4d—£20 (Dedham).

20 *CPR, 1381–85*, 298.

21 Ibid., 317.

22 Ibid., 449.

23 *CFR, 1327–37*, 299; *CPR, 1330–34*, 69. This concession to Robert was to help make up a grant of lands worth £200 a year, a grant in recognition of his part in the arrest of Roger Mortimer and his friends at Nottingham castle in 1330.

24 *CCR, 1381–85*, 53–4.

25 *CFR, 1327–37*, 299.

26 *CPR, 1385–88*, 484; *CCR, 1385–89*, 508.

27 200 m + £10 *minus* £131 8s 5d.

28 *CPR, 1381–85*, 535.

29 Ibid., 67. The annual farm for Haslebury Plucknett laid to the charge of a succession of other custodians answerable to the Exchequer was £42 (1378), £43 6s 8d (February 1387) and £44 (June 1387), (*CFR, 1377–83*, 96; *1383–91*, 172, 188).

30 *Cal. Chartor Rolls, 1341–1417*, 281, 291, 296.

31 *CPR, 1381–85*, 555.

32 *CFR, 1383–91*, 233.

33 Ibid., 211.

34 *Thomas Walsingham . . . Historia Anglicana*, ed. H. T. Riley (R.S., 1863), II, 69–70.Walsingham elsewhere referred to Scrope as 'vir qui spectabili scientia et inflexibili justitia non haberet ex sua fortuna parem in regno' (ibid., 49).

35 Possibly, Scrope had reasons of his own for reticence on this account: in the course of the suit over his heraldic arms which were counter-claimed by Sir Robert Grosvenor, the suit in which he was currently in 1386 defendant in the Court of Chivalry, doubt had been thrown on his own gentility as son of a 'man of law'. (See E. L. G. Stones, 'Sir Geoffrey le Scrope', *E.H.R.*, XLIX (1954), 8, and note 2.

36 For William's financial career, see E. B. Fryde, 'Edward III's Wool Monopoly of 1337: a Fourteenth Century Royal Trading Venture', *History*, N.S., XXXVII, 8–24; G. O. Sayles, 'The "English Company" of 1343 and a merchant's oath', *Speculum*,

VI, 177–205; E. B. Fryde, 'The English Farmers of the Customs, 1343–51', *Transactions of the Royal Historical Society*, 5th ser., IX, 1–17; E. B. Fryde, 'The Last Trials of Sir William de la Pole', *Economic History Review*, 2nd ser., XV, 17–30.

37 *CPR, 1354–58*, 184.

38 *Historia Anglicana*, II, 146; 141. The two passages quoted may be translated, respectively, as follows: 'the son of a merchant, a merchant himself, from his youth up he had been more occupied in commerce than in the profession of arms'; 'a man better fitted for commerce than for soldiering, and one who had grown old among bankers in peace time, not among men-at-arms in war.'

39 T. Carte, *Rolles Gascons*, etc., II, 57.

40 *The Complete Peerage*, XII, Part I, 437. It was about this time, or not much later, that Michael married Katherine, daughter and heir of Sir John Wingfield, who was the Black Prince's 'chief councillor' and business manager during the last ten years of his life, 1351–61.

41 Ibid.

42 Ibid., 438.

43 By November 1372, for service on this expedition, Lancaster had paid Michael £400 out of wages of war and other charges, all together amounting to £572-odd, these other charges including compensation for captured horses (*John of Gaunt's Register, 1372–76*, II, ed. S. A. Smith, in Royal Historical Society, Camden Third Series, XXI, 99).

44 *Ouevres de Froissart*, ed. K. de Lettenhove, *Chroniques*, VII, 481–2; VIII, 31, 71.

45 In anticipation of this expedition Michael took out royal letters patent of protection on 28 March 1373 (*John of Gaunt's Register*, op. cit., I, 32).

46 *Calendar of Papal Registers, Papal Letters*, IV, 132.

47 Michael was mayor of Hull in 1376–7 (*CCR, 1374–77*, 465; *1377–81*, 86).

48 *Foedera*, III, 1065; IV, 15, 36.

49 Ibid., IV, 60; Carte, op. cit., II, 128.

50 More formal and thorough negotiations, conducted throughout 1380 and in 1381, were not concluded until 1 September 1381 (E. Perroy, *L'Angleterre et le Grand Schisme d'Occident* (Paris, 1933), chapter IV). The evidence of Urban VI's interest in the mission in Germany is confirmed by his provision of Michael's son John to the prebend of Wistow in the cathedral church of York (ratified in England on 8 March 1381), expressly in consideration of Michael's losses on the embassy, particularly

those arising from his capture, imprisonment, and payment of a large ransom (*CPR, 1377–81*, 610). For the origins of Rome's rivalry with the Avignonese anti-pope, see pp. 41–2.

51 Perroy, op. cit., 153–4.
52 *John of Gaunt's Register, 1379–83*, ed. Eleanor C. Lodge and R. Somerville, Royal Historical Society, Camden Third Series, LVII, 293; Carte, op. cit., II, 130.
53 P.R.O., Exchequer, Foreign Accounts, E 364/14, D.
54 F. Devon, *Issues of the Exchequer* (London, 1837), 224.
55 *Rot. Parl.*, III, 104b. See above, p. 30.
56 *CCR, 1385–89*, 136, 151.
57 P.R.O., Exchequer K.R., E101, bundle 96, no. 15.
58 *Rot. Parl.*, III, 242b.
59 *Historia Anglicana*, II, 141.
60 Ibid., 146. See pp. 72–4.
61 *Chronicon Henrici Knighton* . . ., ed. J. R. Lumby (R.S. 1895), II, 211.
62 *Rot. Parl.*, III, 168–70.
63 *CCR, 1381–85*, 468, 610.
64 It is possible that William de Ufford and Michael de la Pole were cousins, sons of sisters (or daughters) of Sir Walter de Norwich, Chief Baron of the Exchequer at his death in 1329; but if this were so, little if any account can have been taken of it. (See *D.N.B.*, XIV, 672, 674, and XVI, 50. But cf. *Complete Peerage*, XII, Part I, 437.) If Dugdale (*Baronage*, II, 182) is right in saying that Michael's mother was a daughter and not a sister of *Sir John* de Norwich, it was she who was Ufford's cousin, not Michael.
65 *Historia Anglicana*, II, 49.
66 There is chronicle evidence that the day of Richard II's entry into Scotland (6 August 1385), when Edmund of Langley and Thomas of Woodstock were promoted to dukedoms and Michael de la Pole was made an earl, also saw the creation of John, lord Neville of Raby, as earl of Cumberland and of Sir Simon de Burley as earl of Huntingdon, the Westminster Chronicle recording the first of these two additional promotions (*Polychronicon Ranulphi Higden*, ed. J. R. Lumby, IX [R.S. 1886], 64), Henry Knighton, the second (*Chronicon*, ed. J. R. Lumby, II [R.S. 1895], 205). Neither of these two promotions was confirmed in the parliament which met on 20 October following. Indeed, Neville appears, in the record of the writs of summons issued on 3 September, listed among the barons (as previously), and Burley not at all. (For reasons why these two

promotions may nevertheless be considered to have taken place, see J. J. N. Palmer, 'The Parliament of 1385 and the Constitutional Crisis of 1386', *Speculum*, XLVI (1971), Appendix, 489–90). A further point of interest is that Thomas of Woodstock was formally summoned to the parliament as duke of Albemarle, not Gloucester (as always afterwards). There may, indeed, have been some original confusion as to which new ducal title not only Thomas, but also his brother Edmund should take. Regarding Edmund, the Westminster Chronicle says that he was promoted from earl to duke of *Cambridge*, not York, and regarding Thomas, who was earl of Buckingham, merely that he was promoted 'in ducem' (i.e. without specifying the new title). It may also be noted that on 2 December, near the end of the parliament, Robert de Vere, earl of Oxford, was created marquess of Dublin.

67 *Rot. Parl.*, III, 206–7.
68 Ibid., 207–8.
69 The queen and the countess held their lands 'per separabiles quantitates'.
70 Michael did in fact predecease the two ladies: he died on 5 September 1389, the queen on 7 June 1394, and the dowager countess Isabel on 29 September 1416.
71 It was no later than 25 September 1385 that the king, having taken Thomas's homage and fealty, gave him livery of seisin of their mother's lands, with all the issues from the time of her death (*CFR, 1383–91*, 123).
72 As in note 68.
73 *CPR, 1385–89*, 18.
74 *Rot. Parl.*, III, 208–9; *CPR, 1385–89*, 24.
75 From Lowestoft and Wendover.
76 From Marlborough, Barnwell priory and Winchester.
77 *CPR, 1385–89*, 156.
78 Ibid., 530.
79 Ibid., *1377–81*, 450–1.
80 *Rot. Parl.*, III, 207b.
81 Ibid., 208b.
82 *CPR, 1338–40*, 265.
83 *CFR, 1327–37*, 215.
84 *CPR, 1334–38*, 418.
85 Here is an apparent discrepancy, perhaps a contradiction: if we subtract the value of Haughley in 1339 (£126-odd) from the combined value of Eye and Haughley in 1330 (£373), we have Eye then seemingly worth about £247; whereas if we assume (for want of other evidence, and for the sake of argument) that

Thorndon was worth in 1337 what it was valued at in 1382
(£35) and subtract that from the combined value of Eye and
Thorndon in 1337 (£207-odd), Eye was then seemingly worth
only about £172. The difference in the apparent approximate
values of Eye in 1330 and 1337—one of about £75—is too wide
for either value to be credible. Neither figure is acceptable for
comparison with that of 1382 (£200).

86 *CPR, 1396–99*, 359.
87 *CPR, 1327–30*, 67; *1334–38*, 418; *1338–40*, 265; *CFR, 1327–37*, 389.
88 *CPR, 1327–30*, 67.
89 Ibid., *1381–85*, 567.
90 Ibid., *1327–30*, 519.
91 Ibid., *1334–38*, 418.
92 *CCR, 1349–54*, 113.
93 *CPR, 1327–30*, 272.
94 Ibid., *1374–77*, 347, 367.
95 Ibid., *1377–81*, 84–5.
96 Ibid., *1374–77*, 474–5.
97 Ibid., 367.
98 Ibid., *1377–81*, 441.
99 *Rot. Parl.*, III, 205–6.
100 *CPR, 1385–89*, 62.
101 *CCR, 1385–89*, 198. Not until 23 March 1387 was Edmund given any land in aid of his dukedom (the manor of Hitchen, Herts., worth £100 a year) (*CPR, 1385–89*, 292).
102 *CCR, 1377–81*, 390.
103 *CPR, 1377–81*, 60.
104 Ibid., 372.
105 *CCR, 1385–89*, 224.
106 *Rot. Parl.*, III, 206.
107 *CPR, 1385–89*, 55.
108 Ibid., 147.
109 Ibid., 209. It was only after the forfeitures of the 'Merciless Parliament' of 1388 that, from the lands of Robert de Vere, Michael de la Pole, and others, then condemned for treason, Thomas of Woodstock received estates worth £2,000 a year (£1,000 for the earldom of Buckingham, £1,000 for the dukedom of Gloucester) (*CPR, 1385–89*, 479).
110 For Thomas of Woodstock's endowments by royal grant and his difficulties in realising upon them, compare Anthony Goodman, *The Loyal Conspiracy. The Lords Appellant under Richard II* (London, 1971), 90–2, and Anthony Tuck, *Richard II and the English Nobility* (London, 1973), 101–2, 128.

111 Regarding the impeachment as a whole, however, there is good reason to believe that the Commons were acting independently. The charges against De la Pole were consistent with their general line of criticism of the government in this period. Nor were they 'credulous and willing to be led' (as H. G. Richardson once asserted); still less were they subservient. That the Commons were acting independently of the Upper House in 1386 is surely made clear by the fact that, although the Lords adjudicated favourably upon some of the articles of impeachment (those relating to Michael's peculations), there were other articles (those relating to his official acts as chancellor) upon which they did not. Touching this question of 'inspiration', it would be very helpful to know by whom, and at whose behest, were discovered, in the Chancery and Exchequer records, those facts which related to the charges made against Michael, and were put at the Commons' disposal. But, then, we do not know.

XI

The fourth article

(paraphrasing the parliament-roll)

This fourth charge of Michael's impeachment[1] was that, although aware that an inheritable income of £50 a year from the customs of Hull granted by Edward III to one Tidemann of Limburg had been forfeited, and payment of it discontinued for twenty or thirty years, he had nonetheless procured from the present king, to whom was due all benefit from the forfeiture, a confirmation of the 'purchase' he had once made of that annuity from Tidemann.

In his initial answer,[2] Michael explained that Tidemann's annuity, perpetually inheritable from the first and (as demonstrable by accounts rendered in the Exchequer by the Hull collectors of the 'ancient custom') actually paid for a considerable period, had long ago, by a deed of Edward III's reign, been transferred to him, similarly as a perpetual inheritance, in return for the cancellation of a debt of 1,000 marks Tidemann owed him; that in view of his having surrendered Tidemann's letters patent, and acquitted the king of all arrears of the grant, he was given a royal pardon of the purchase; and that he was ignorant then, as he still was, of any forfeiture, or debt, to the king on Tidemann's part.

The Commons' reply[3] was: to suggest that record evidence that Tidemann was greatly indebted to the king would probably be discovered in the Exchequer; to assert that, even if the income in question had not been forfeit for other reasons, it therefore belonged to the king, who consequently had been the victim of a deception; and then to request an investigation of the records. And (referring to a particular cause of forfeiture) they added that one Neil ('Neel') Hackney had been done to death by his wife, a servant and Tidemann, as a result of which the wife and the servant had been executed by burning, Tidemann having fled.

The Commons, when referring to the king's having been deceived, were not simply claiming that, because Tidemann had been heavily in debt to the Crown, the king was being defrauded of an income of £50 a year (the annuity which Edward III had granted to Tidemann, and which Tidemann had transferred to Michael). They were doing much else besides, a fact that emerges only in the report of Michael's rejoinder (his recorded submission on this point being, however, amplified and clarified in the final judgment). For what Michael now sought to rebut was evidently a further accusation: that, after being confirmed in possession of the annuity, he had gone on to exchange it for a manor worth four times as much, namely, the manor of Faxfleet in the East Riding of Yorkshire, which was worth, so the Commons alleged, £200 a year.[4] This accusation also, therefore, was two-edged: not only was Michael accused of yet again converting an income leviable upon customs revenue into one that was derived from landed estate, but also of yet again securing landed estate that had been undervalued, even grossly undervalued, thus enabling him to make an additional personal gain, and to involve the Crown in a further loss *pro tanto*.

It was only this latter point of undervaluation which, as would appear from the record of the parliament-roll, Michael challenged.[5] What he said in rebuttal was that one Sir William de Murrers had told him that, having taken out a seven years' lease of two thirds of the manor of Faxfleet and a rent in North Dalton (East Riding) worth ten marks in exchange for an annual payment of fifty marks, he had incurred an overall loss of 100 marks in the course of his tenure; and also that there was an extent in the Chancery which valued the whole manor and rent at no more than £41 9s 3½d. However, understanding the earl of Kent to have later held the two thirds of the manor and rent as again worth fifty marks a year, Michael had himself taken them at the same valuation. Moreover, he insisted that they were not worth more, or even as much, adding that if anyone was ready to meet the necessary expenses ('charges') of the manor and pay him fifty marks a year for the two thirds or, when the remaining third should become available, £50 for the entire manor and rent, he would arrange it very willingly ('de bone coer').

The judgment regarding this article[6] was concerned, firstly, with the question as to whether Tidemann's transfer of the annuity of £50 charged on the Hull customs had been legally permissible, and whether the king had been the victim of a deception when, subsequently, Michael obtained a pardon for the transfer and its confirmation; and, secondly, with the question as to whether Michael, in later effecting an exchange of the annuity for the manor of Faxfleet and a rent of ten marks from North Dalton, had done his duty by the king. In both instances, the judgment awarded went against Michael, and, in order to justify it, fresh considerations were adduced. Regarding the legality of the transfer, it was pointed out that the annuity had been granted to Tidemann as a charge on no other source of revenue save the 'ancient custom' levied in the port of Hull. There was doubt, too, as to Tidemann's continued enjoyment of the grant: he was a foreigner (as was well known) and had not now been resident in the kingdom for over thirty years; nor was it alleged that any agent of his had laid claim to the annuity for a long time. Besides, Tidemann had in no wise been entitled to alienate the annuity without (prior) royal agreement, seeing that it had been granted only to him and his *heirs* (as was plain from his charter as recorded), not to him and his *assignees*. Then again, Michael had failed to show that his purchase of the annuity had been effected in England, with the result that it had not been possible to ascertain whether or not that transaction was legally sound ('bone et legale'). Nor had Michael maintained in his answer that, when procuring the royal pardon and confirmation of the transfer, he had made it abundantly clear to the king that the annuity could be retained by the Crown, at least until it was demanded by Tidemann or his lineal heirs (provided these had been born subjects of the king, and were known). On all these grounds, and also because the grant of the pardon and confirmation required a large fine, whereas none had been imposed, it was apparent that the king had been deceived. Regarding the exchange, by royal concession, of the annuity levied on the 'ancient custom' collected at Hull for the manor of Faxfleet and ten marks of rent from North Dalton, it was emphasised in the award[7] that, whereas the earlier source of income was precarious, in that either the port might be destroyed by the sea or the export of wool (on which collection of the 'ancient custom' depended) be unsettled or ruined, income from the later source was certain and assured. But in any case, because Michael, in his answer, did not prove that, in accepting by exchange the manor and rent as a good and perfect means of securing the income due from the annuity, he had discharged his responsibility to the king, that answer must be accounted insufficient to exonerate him from the offence imputed.

The substance of the judgment, as distinct from the reasons for the award, was that Michael's charter of pardon and confirmation of the purchase of Tidemann's annuity of £50 should be revoked and annulled, and the income represented by the annuity retained in future by the king; that the manor of Faxfleet and the ten marks' rent should similarly be resumed; and that Michael should forfeit all the income he had received from either the annuity or the manor and rent, this sum to be levied upon his lands and chattels, to the king's use.

The story which lies behind this fourth charge regarding Tidemann of Limburg's £50 annuity, and Michael's acquisition and alleged exploitation of it, is both complicated and, at times, obscure; but at least its beginning and end are clear enough. No difficulty presents itself as to the origin of the £50 annuity Tidemann transferred to Michael. Curiously, Tidemann's own interest in the annuity had begun as the result of another, earlier transfer.[8] This had taken place on 15 February 1344, when Edward III acceded to a petition from a merchant of Asti, in

Piedmont, who, being heavily in debt to Tidemann and a German business partner of his, John de Wold, but holding a royal annuity of £50 payable out of the wool customs levied in London, requested that it should be consigned to them and their heirs, but as a charge on the 'ancient custom' collected at Hull. By May 1347 Tidemann's partner and co-grantee had died, apparently without heirs since William de la Pole (Michael's father, who had a lien at the time on all the 'ancient custom' at Hull) was then ordered to pay a half-yearly instalment of the whole annuity of £50 to Tidemann alone.[9] That Tidemann was able to retain the grant in this fashion is hardly surprising, considering his high standing as a merchant banker in England, and his services to the Crown in these middle years of Edward III's reign.

When first made a co-grantee of the annuity in question, Tidemann, who was a subject of the duke of Brabant-Limburg, was one of the very foremost of the German Hansards of the London Steelyard. As such he had headed the consortium which, in return for massive credits in aid of the French war, farmed the English wool customs from May 1340 to March 1344.[10] He again led the German merchants when they helped, very substantially, to finance, first, John Wesenham of Lynn, the farmer of the customs between April 1345 and October 1346, and then two Londoners, Walter Chiriton and Thomas Swanland, who outbid Wesenham and took over the farm until they went bankrupt in April 1349.[11] Moreover, when first paid as sole remaining grantee of the Hull annuity in 1347, Tidemann was already closely connected with the Black Prince. The latter, who was heavily in his debt, had appointed him by November 1346 as his receiver of the 'coinage' of the duchy of Cornwall and sole agent for buying and exporting Cornish tin,[12] and had then, in June 1347, allowed him, at an annual farm of 3,500 marks, a lease of the stannary of the duchy, a lease which, although the contract initially was to end at Michaelmas 1350, lasted until 1352.[13] It was in this year that the English farmers of the customs were subjected to proceedings in the Exchequer for failing to fulfil their engagements with the king; and

Tidemann himself was so directly involved in the suit
brought by the Crown for repayment of the farmers' debts,
which amounted to 13,000 marks, as to be twice put into the
Tower. Not until July 1354 was he finally disembarrassed of
the outcome of the prosecution, but by then, following the
king's agreement a year before to reduce the farmers' debt to
9,000 marks, he had paid his personal share of it.[14] Thereafter, it was only on a relatively small scale that Tidemann
was ever again implicated in financial business with Edward
III. (The same was true of the German merchants of the
Steelyard generally.) Bearing in mind, however, the Commons' allegations in 1386 that, when Tidemann left England
for good, he was still so greatly indebted to the king as to
have forfeited all right to the £50 annuity which he eventually
transferred to Michael de la Pole, it is important to record
that not only did the Exchequer, in May 1355, certify that he
was clear of all debt to the Crown,[15] but also the royal
Council, in November 1367, certified that the king was free
of all debt to him.[16] The latter note rather suggests that any
indebtedness is more likely to have persisted on Edward III's
part than Tidemann's, or at least makes it extremely doubtful
that Tidemann had ever forfeited the £50 annuity because of
some heavy residual indebtedness to the king. Certainly,
when the Commons said in 1386 that that forfeiture had
involved a discontinuance of payment of the annuity for
twenty or thirty years, they were guilty of an exaggeration.
Neither the date of Tidemann's final departure from England,[17] nor that of his transfer of the annuity to Michael, is
known, but payments of the annuity to Tidemann himself
continued to be recorded in the customs accounts for Hull
until 1368.[18] However, the Commons had not only alleged in
1386 that the annuity had been forfeited because of large
unpaid debts to the Crown, and that payment had been
discontinued for that reason: the annuity, they urged, would
have been forfeit in any case, meaning on account of
Tidemann's incrimination in the murder of Neil Hackney,
'for which felony he had fled'.

Neil Hackney, a citizen of London, the son of a former woolmonger and alderman, and himself the owner of the manor of Badmangore in Kent and of property in Stepney, seemingly met his death in 1352.[19] Certainly, it was in Easter term 1353 that his brother Richard brought an appeal for his murder before the court of the King's Bench. According to the judicial record, those appealed were Hermann Mynter (a German Hanseatic merchant), William de Kirkley, and the victim's wife's mother (Juliana, wife of John Hardyngham); but Kirkley did not appear, and the other two were acquitted. Nothing more is known save that, when the suit was reopened, it was once more against Mynter and Kirkley, neither of whom could be found. Tidemann is known to have been a business associate of Mynter's, but in the record of neither trial is his name even mentioned, and, in fact, no other evidence than the Commons' imputation of over thirty years later has been discovered connecting him with the crime.[20] Nor is it that he was absent from England: indeed, at the time of the first trial he was undergoing prosecution by the Exchequer and, moreover, on 10 June 1353, while that first trial was still on, he was summoned, along with three other German and some English merchants, to confer with the Council a fortnight later.[21] Then again, his later activities and dealings in England seem hardly to consort with incrimination in any murder, still less with his conviction.

Tidemann, however, is mentioned in 1377, shortly before Edward III's death, as having committed a 'misprision and offence' previously resulting in the escheat of lands leased to him by the Cluniac priory of Bermondsey, lands which the king was then restoring to it.[22] The misdemeanour referred to has not been traced, but the word 'misprision' usually indicates an offence of some gravity, and a misdemeanour serious enough to have resulted in the escheat of Tidemann's Bermondsey priory lands, whether or not it led also to his fleeing the country, might well have involved him in the forfeiture of other possessions, including perhaps the Hull annuity of £50. But what we also do not know is whether, if Tidemann did incur a more general forfeiture, the transfer of the annuity to Michael de la Pole had or had not preceded it (although the Commons in 1386 evidently believed the transfer to have postdated it). Lacking clear evidence, then, it must remain an open question whether Tidemann, when transferring the annuity, had granted something he still possessed or something that was no longer his to give away. But this is, of course, to leave all on one side the objection, referred to only in the judgment in Michael's trial, that Tidemann's own original grant of the annuity had been one made to him and his *heirs*, not to him and his *assignees*, an objection which in any case would seem to have been unanswerable. The immediate reason for the transfer of the annuity to Michael is also obscure: the debt of 1,000 marks which, Michael said, Tidemann owed him and he himself had waived as a condition of his purchase of the annuity. This particular debt cannot be identified, but relations between Tidemann and the De la Poles as a family had always been close (witness especially Tidemann's conveyance to Michael and his brothers in 1354 of a large portion of the English estates of the Norman abbey of Grestain),[23] and there is no reason to question the fact of the debt. But all that is known for sure of the transfer is that it was transacted, without benefit of royal licence, some time between 1368 (until when the annuity had continued to be paid to Tidemann himself) and the end of Edward III's reign. It may also be reasonably presumed that no payment of the annuity was ever made from the time of the transfer until Michael's bargain with Tidemann was ratified by Richard II. If this was so, then Michael *ipso facto* virtually obtained a source of personal income which previously had been only putative, and which he had never actually enjoyed. He was chancellor when he did so.

The ratification in question occurred at Reading on 15 May 1385, Tidemann's original grant being then surrendered.[24] It took shape in letters patent under the great seal (warranted by writ of privy seal), these not only regularising the transfer, but also conceding that Michael and his heirs might ultimately derive the income in question (£50 a year) from lands or rents.

Actually on the day of issue of the letters patent, letters close were addressed to the collectors of the Hull customs authorising them to pay the annuity.[25] Then, at Newcastle upon Tyne on 20 August following (a fortnight after Michael's promotion to the earldom of Suffolk, and on the day of his main royal grant of financial support for his new rank), Michael procured, in return for a cancellation of the grant of 15 May, and in lieu of two thirds of the £50 annuity, a grant in fee simple, under the great seal (again warranted by writ of privy seal), of the two thirds of the manor of Faxfleet and the rent of ten marks in North Dalton held until recently (8 August, the date of the king's mother's death) by the king's half-brother, Thomas Holland, earl of Kent, and previously extended at £41 9s 3½d a year; and in the same grant Michael also secured the reversion of the other third of the manor and rent, which then happened to be held in dower (by Jacqueline, widow of Sir John de Stirling, and her present husband, Robert de Clifford), he retaining in the meantime a third of the original £50 annuity as a charge on the Hull customs as before.[26] Finally, at Stamford on 3 September following, Michael covered himself against foreseeable future contingencies by obtaining, again in letters under the great seal, a grant of the whole manor of Faxfleet up to the value of £50 a year (any surplus to be remitted to the Exchequer),[27] a grant which, because of the continuance of Jacqueline's tenure in dower beyond the time of his forfeiture in 1386, he was never able to enjoy.[28]

As we have seen, all Michael's grants of the £50 annuity made in 1385 were subsequently to be impugned on the ground that they had originated in Tidemann's transfer, a transaction that was illegal because none but Tidemann's heirs had ever been entitled to succeed him in possession, and even more obviously invalid because Tidemann, having incurred forfeiture, could not alienate what he himself no longer possessed. Michael's own admission in his trial that he had been pardoned for the transfer and, in order to obtain the pardon, had been ready to acquit the king of all arrears of the annuity, tends to confirm the imputation. But what the Commons doubtless most strongly objected to was that, in exchange for an annuity deriving from a source of royal revenue (the customs) which, given the exigencies of the export trade and Exchequer assignments competing for such revenue, was notoriously insecure, Michael had obtained instead, temporarily in great part, prospectively in whole, a manor and a rent from landed estate; and, with at least equal force, that Michael's offence had been aggravated by his acceptance of an underassessment of the estates in question, the income derived from these being, the Commons insisted, far in excess of the annuity surrendered. What evidence can be found bearing on this particular aspect of the charge?

When a royal grant happened to be made of the manor of Faxfleet, it was usually in combination with a rent from North Dalton, a fixed rent. Whether, when this was the case, such a grant was affected by under- or overassessment obviously depended upon a valuation of the manor alone, and the question of the liability of its value to vary is all that needs to be determined. In fact, such evidence as can be found suggests that the assessments of the annual value of Faxfleet not only fluctuated, but did so quite considerably. For purposes of comparison we may take as our datum the year in which Michael was first given an interest in the income of the manor: 1385. Even then, however, the manor's official annual value was uncertain. The estimate actually accepted, first by Thomas Holland, earl of Kent, and then by Michael, was £43 6s 8d (£50 *minus* ten marks of rent from North Dalton); but Michael, when stating (correctly) that two thirds of manor and rent had also, according to an extent in the Chancery, been estimated at £41 9s 3½d, himself implicitly allowed that the annual income from the entire manor and rent was to be taken as £62 3s 11¼d and that of the manor alone as £55 10s 7¼d. Even in 1385, then, there was a considerable difference between two optional estimates of the worth of Faxfleet: a difference of £12 3s 11¼d. The Commons, however, had gone so far as to allege that the manor was worth £200 a year, a figure nearly four times the larger estimate Michael was prepared to concede. But what of other evidence?

When the manor of Faxfleet, having been forfeited by the Templars, finally came into Crown possession in 1324, it had immediately been absorbed into a complex of estates tied to the financial support of the King's Chamber,[29] and was soon to become the subject of grants to one and then another important member of the royal Household. When granted in 1327 to John Wysham (who in the following year became steward of the Household) its annual value was put at £51.[30] But when, in 1332, it was given for life to the then steward, Ralph, lord Neville of Raby, it was extended at only £39 7s 8d a year.[31] Despite the discovery in 1339 of certain 'alienations and withdrawals' which in the next year were together estimated at £10 6s 1½d a year[32] and, had an intention to resume them been fulfilled, would obviously have restored the annual value of the manor to nearly £50, an extent of May 1343, valuing the manor at £39 11s,[33] almost exactly confirmed the estimate of 1332. However, in December 1343, when the reversion of the manor and (now for the first time associated with it) the rent of ten marks from North Dalton was entailed upon Sir John de Stirling,[34] the manor, following further enquiries, was held to be worth £54 12s a year[35] (the manor and the rent combined, £61 5s 4d). This estimate was as good as confirmed in 1367, when Lord Neville died and, under the reversion, Stirling was given livery of seisin: the manor was then taken to be yielding £55 a year.[36] With it, Stirling evidently also obtained the North Dalton rent of ten marks (as, of course, he was entitled), for on 5 November 1378, following Stirling's recent death,[37] it was ordered that a third of both manor and rent be assigned in dower to his widow Jacqueline (Jacoba). The royal escheator in Yorkshire was instructed to arrange for this in the presence of Sir William de Murrers,[38] a knight of the King's Chamber, to whose tale of his disappointing experiences as farmer of the remaining two thirds of the manor and rent Michael referred (it will be recalled) at his trial. In part, but only in small part, that tale is confirmed by the Chancery records. On 2 November 1378, and so briefly anticipating the order to give Stirling's widow seisin of her estate in dower, Murrers had secured the custody, for seven years (as from Stirling's death), of the remaining two thirds of the manor and rent, on condition of meeting the costs of upkeep and paying the Exchequer a rent of fifty marks a year.[39] Evidently, the official annual value of the whole manor and rent had fallen back to £50, and at this figure it still remained on 6 June 1381, when the two thirds were assigned (as worth fifty marks) to Thomas Holland, earl of Kent.[40] But here, arising out of this grant to Kent, is, implicitly, a complication which has a bearing on the validity of Michael de la Pole's reference at his trial to Murrers's experience as farmer, indeed a double bearing, partly confirmatory, partly contradictory. This grant to Kent must have depended upon Murrers surrendering his farm. If that surrender had been voluntary, it could be taken as indirectly supporting Michael's reference to Murrers's dissatisfaction with a contract which (so, Michael said, Murrers had told him) had brought him only a loss. But the loss had been stated to be one of as much as 100 marks, and yet it now appears that Murrers had held the farm not for seven years (as he initially intended), but for no more than about three.[41] So great a loss over so short a period is hardly credible: given the total sum of the renders to the Exchequer, and given the recurrent fixed income from the North Dalton rent, the income from the manor itself is left impossibly low;[42] and, in any case, the difference it presupposes between the real income from the manor and rent and its official valuation, a valuation Michael was himself prepared to agree, is too large a difference to be acceptable. On the basis of this analysis, Michael's reference to Murrers's experience as a predecessor, although apparently not challenged at his trial, was ill-conceived.

Reviewing the previous sixty years' history of the officially recognised income of the whole manor of Faxfleet and, whenever the ten marks' rent from North Dalton happens *not* to have been associated with it, including this rent in the calculation all the same (in order consistently to compare like with like), it must be conceded that the valuation of £50 accepted by Michael in 1385 did not differ radically from earlier ones: the lowest of these had been £46 1s (1332); the highest (if we "gross up" the valuation of £41 9s 3½d for the two thirds which was referred to in Michael's patent and mentioned by him at his trial), £62 3s 11¼d. This latter valuation considerably exceeded (by nearly twenty-five per cent) the £50 estimate which, adopted as the basis of the most recent grant previous to his own (the earl of Kent's), Michael had preferred as the more profitable to himself. But £62-odd is still short of even a third of the way towards the £200 of the Commons' estimate of Faxfleet, etc. Were the Commons really so far out? Admittedly when, on 20 November 1387, following Michael's forfeiture of his grant, the two thirds of Faxfleet and the North Dalton rent were leased out afresh, to David Holgrave, king's esquire, the annual farm Holgrave was to render at the Exchequer was only fifty-five marks,[43] indicating that the value of the whole manor and rent was still officially regarded as no higher than £55. However, on 28 February 1392, when the king made a grant in fee simple to Henry, lord Scrope of Masham, of the entire manor and rent along with £20 from the fee-farm of Hull, this was in return for the surrender of an annuity of 200 marks payable at the Exchequer.[44] Provided Lord Scrope's recompense was a fair one, this would mean that the manor of Faxfleet was itself now thought to be worth 160 marks a year, and the manor and rent combined 170 marks (£113 6s 8d),[45] which, although still far short of the Commons' estimate of £200, is moving up in that direction. Obviously, the Commons' estimate had exaggerated; but perhaps not so inordinately as other, earlier evidence would seem to indicate.

To sum up. At bottom, the Commons' accusation contained in the fourth charge was that Michael, when chancellor, had deceived the king into allowing him an income to which he was not entitled, so involving the Crown in an unnecessary financial loss. And the justification for this basic charge was threefold: (1) because Tidemann of Limburg had forfeited the £50 annuity on the Hull customs, his transfer of it to Michael ought never to have been made and was invalid, and it was not until when, long afterwards, Michael became chancellor, that he made any effort to assert and realise upon his claim; (2) when Michael exchanged the annuity for landed estate, he was substituting a source of income naturally assured for one naturally uncertain; and (3) he had profited from this transaction additionally, for the landed estate in question, being grossly underassessed, was worth far more than the annuity surrendered. Regarding (1): although the Commons' assertions on the score of Tidemann's long non-enjoyment of the annuity and his forfeiture of it for debt and incrimination in a felony cannot be factually substantiated, it is possible that Michael, aware of the necessity for a royal pardon regularising the transfer of the annuity, but delaying his request until a favourable opportunity presented itself, was himself doubtful of the legality of the transfer. Regarding (2): the facts of the case being what they were, no defence was possible against this accusation. Regarding (3): all ascertainable evidence relating to the previous officially estimated annual worth of the manor of Faxfleet and the rent of ten marks from North Dalton combined, suggests that, while sometimes less than £50 (the value of the annuity exchanged), the income was more frequently in excess of that amount, although in absolute terms never (until some years later) by very much; but it would appear that, if the Commons exaggerated in their estimate of £200 as the value of the manor and rent, Michael also went too far in stressing at his trial the dissatisfaction felt by a recent farmer of the property (Sir William de Murrers) who, allegedly, had found an Exchequer rent of fifty marks a year for two thirds of it exorbitant. Michael himself admitted to the property being more valuable than was presupposed by the exchange. What, however, is nowhere mentioned in the record of the trial is that, in his final grant of the whole manor and rent (the grant made at Stamford on 5 September 1385, which would become effective only when the existing dower rights of Jacqueline de Stirling to a third of the property ceased), Michael had undertaken to remit to the Exchequer any income surplus to £50, a condition which might have been taken to mitigate the force of this particular accusation. However that may be, Michael had secured a ratification of Tidemann's transfer of the annuity; in so doing he had obtained an income which he had not previously enjoyed; and he soon converted the source of that income from customs revenue to landed estate. It is questionable whether he would have been able to do any of these things, still less all of them, had he not been chancellor at the time.

Notes

1 *Rot. Parl.*, III, 216a.
2 Ibid., 217b.
3 Ibid., 218a.
4 Ibid., 218b. Faxfleet (East Riding) is situated on the north bank of the mouth of the R. Ouse, directly opposite the confluence of the R. Trent, and had long been used as a port by the merchants of York.
5 *Rot. Parl.*, III, 218b–219a, North Dalton (East Riding) is on the edge of the Wolds, roughly seven miles south-west of Great Driffield.
6 *Rot. Parl.*, III, 219b.
7 Ibid., 220a.
8 *CPR, 1343–45*, 211.
9 *CCR, 1346–49*, 206.
10 Ibid., *1339–41*, 483–4; *1343–46*, 287.
11 E. B. Fryde, 'The English Farmers of the Customs, 1343–51', *T.R.H.S.*, 5th ser., IX (1959), 4, 5.
12 *Register of Edward, the Black Prince* (H.M.S.O.), Part I, 32, 121.
13 *CPR, 1345–48*, 373. The monopoly conferred by the lease met with an early protest in the parliament of January 1348 (*Rot. Parl.*, II, 168a). It was a Bodmin merchant who was buying the prince's tin by June 1353 (*Black Prince's Register*, Part II, 48).
14 Alice Beardwood, *Alien Merchants in England: their legal and economic position 1350 to 1377* (Cambridge [Mass.], 1931), 18–9.
15 *CPR, 1354–58*, 217.
16 Ibid., *1367–70*, 36.
17 At least occasionally, Tidemann was in Dortmund between 1356 and 1370. He purchased a house in Cologne, becoming a burgess there in 1371. He died in 1386, and was buried in the church of the hermits of St Augustine in that city (Beardwood, 21).
18 Beardwood, 21. The last specific order to pay a half-yearly instalment which actually passed the great seal and was enrolled on the close roll of the Chancery is dated 8 November 1363

(*CCR*, *1360–64*, 493), such orders having previously issued with perfect regularity in 1347–8, only intermittently thereafter (in 1350, 1352 and 1362).

19 It was on 14 September 1352 that the guardianship of Neil's only child, Alice, was entrusted by the mayor and aldermen of London to her uncle, Sir Thomas Moraunt of Kent (*Calendars of Letter Books of the City of London: Letter Books A–G*, ed. R. R. Sharpe (London, 1899–1905), *Letter Book F*, 248.

20 Beardwood, 20.

21 *CCR*, *1349–54*, 605.

22 *CPR*, *1374–77*, 480. Cf. *Annales Monastici*, ed. H. R. Luard (R.S. 1866), III, 479.

23 See the Appendix.

24 *CPR*, *1381–85*, 570.

25 *CCR*, *1381–85*, 542.

26 *CPR*, *1385–89*, 32. 'Stirling' is invariably spelt 'Strevylin', 'Strivelin', or the like, in contemporary documents.

27 *CPR*, *1385–89*, 10.

28 Jacqueline (Jacoba), lady Stirling, did in fact outlive Michael de la Pole, dying only shortly before 20 February 1391 (*CFR*, *1383–91*, 360).

29 *CFR*, *1319–27*, 259. *CPR*, *1354–58*, 153; *1377–81*, 444.

30 *CPR*, *1327–30*, 127.

31 *CFR*, *1327–37*, 335.

32 *CPR*, *1338–40*, 272, 494; *CCR*, *1339–41*, 470–1.

33 *Calendar of Inquisitions, Miscellaneous (Chancery)*, II, 461, no. 1852.

34 Stirling, formerly Edward III's constable of Edinburgh castle, was soon to become keeper of Berwick-upon-Tweed.

35 *CPR*, *1343–45*, 159.

36 *CCR*, *1364–68*, 356.

37 Stirling had died before (but probably not long before) 28 August 1378 when the first writs of *diem clausit extremum* issued (*CCR*, *1377–81*, 157).

38 Murrers, whose home was at Elmington (Yorkshire), was now about fifty-six years old. As a young soldier he is known to have served Edward III in his expedition to Antwerp (1335) and at the siege of Tournai (1340). Later, he was at the siege of Paris and the peace-making at Brétigny (1360), and, as a member of John of Gaunt's retinue, he fought at the battle of Najera in Spain (1367). At the time of the grant of 1378 he was constable of Northampton castle, and by June 1381 was marshal of the royal Household. He remained a knight of the King's Chamber until certainly 1390. In the meantime, on 19 September 1386 (only a few weeks before

Michael de la Pole's trial), at St Mary's abbey, York, he had been a witness in favour of Richard, lord Scrope, in the latter's dispute with Sir Robert Grosvenor over their heraldic arms, and it is to his deposition on that occasion that we owe our knowledge of his age and the facts of his earlier military career. (*The Scrope and Grosvenor Controversy*, ed. N. H. Nicolas, I, 135; II, 337–8. See also Tout, *Chapters*, IV, 345).

39 *CFR*, *1377–83*, 112.

40 *CPR*, *1381–85*, 14; cf. ibid., *1377–81*, 450.

41 From Stirling's death in the summer of 1378 until June 1381, when the earl of Kent took over.

42 If for roughly three years Murrers had paid the Exchequer about 150 marks (fifty marks for each year's farm) and ended up with a loss of 100 marks, all that the two thirds of the manor and North Dalton rent had yielded him in the meantime was fifty marks, of which twenty marks ($\frac{2}{3} \times 10$ m $\times$ 3) had derived from the rent, leaving no more than thirty marks to have been contributed by the two thirds of the manor, i.e. ten marks a year, an absurdly low amount.

43 *CFR*, *1383–91*, 201–2.

44 *CPR*, *1391–96*, 66. This annuity of 200 marks had first been given to Henry lord Scrope's father, Geoffrey, Edward III's chief justice of the King's Bench, and his heirs, and in 1362 renewed in Henry's favour (ibid., *1361–64*, 272), Geoffrey having died so long ago as 1340 (See E. L. G. Stones, art. cit.).

45 I.e. 200 marks minus the £20 (30 marks) from the Hull fee farm.

XII

The fifth article

(paraphrasing the parliament-roll)

The fifth article of Michael's impeachment[1] pointed out that whereas the head of the Order ('le haut mestre') of St Anthony of Vienne was a schismatic[2] and, accordingly, the king ought to have enjoyed the yield from the Order's English assets ('le profit'), Michael, whose official duty as chancellor it had been to procure and promote the king's financial advantage, had himself acquired that source of income at an annual farm rent of twenty marks and so benefited by something like 1,000 marks. Moreover, it was added that, when the present master of the English preceptory of the Order should have been given possession of those assets and the London Hospital of St Anthony, they were withheld until, by recognisance and bonds for £3,000 entered into in Chancery, he and two others had undertaken to make an annual payment of £100 to Michael and his son John for the term of their two lives.

Michael's first answer to the charge as recorded[3] provides further evidence of what was in question. He explained that it was before he became chancellor that he requested Richard II to bestow the Hospital or 'procuracy' of St Anthony in England upon his son John. This the king did, and the grant, warranted by a writ to the keeper of the privy seal, was to be free of encumbrances, and with no payment or other condition attached. The keeper of the privy seal, however, in view of the fact that a church was appropriated to the Hospital, was at first unwilling to warrant the grant without a definite farm rent being made payable to the king, but issued the warrant when this stipulation was met, the rent agreed being one of twenty marks a year for the duration of the war with France. Michael said that at that time he was ignorant of the value of the Hospital or procuracy, and that as soon as he realised that it was worth 400 marks a year he informed the king to that effect, only for the latter to reply that, even if it were worth more, he would be well pleased for him to have it all. Michael, moreover, had insisted that, since the receipts would derive, not from a form of temporal or spiritual property, but from moneys collected for pardons ('coillett de Pardon'), he would prefer not to take the income for his own private gain; rather, if it pleased the king, he would devote it to charity ('en almoigne'), an offer to which, in fact, the king agreed. Seeing, therefore, that he had clearly revealed the value of the grant to the king, who had gone on to consent to the bestowal of its proceeds on alms (with the result that he himself had enjoyed no temporal benefit), it was obvious that the king had not been deceived. Michael then proceeded, additionally, to make protestation that his impeachment did not oblige him to answer to the party (i.e. the present master of the Hospital). Nevertheless, in order to explain his position ('son estat'), he went on to state that because the benefice was a spiritual entity, he sent to the pope (Urban VI) to obtain the collation of his son; that the pope granted his request, on condition that his son was professed in the Order within a limited period; that, when this proved impossible, and application was being made to the Roman Curia for a dispensation, all was in suspense; and that the present master then appeared with other (and contradictory) papal bulls of provision relating to the Hospital and, after talks which resulted in Michael's abandoning his suit in the Curia on his son's behalf, willingly granted to them, as a recompense, the annuity of £100 mentioned in the charge.

Evidently dissatisfied with Michael's explanation of the origin of this annuity, the Commons next adverted to the precedent supplied by what had happened to William de Thorpe, a former chief justice of the King's Bench now deceased,[4] who, convicted of taking £20 from one of the parties involved in a plea brought before him, had been deemed to have 'sold law' and, accordingly, adjudged to death and the forfeiture of his goods and chattels. And the Commons continued: in that Michael, when chancellor, had taken the £100 annuity from the present master as papal provisor before making livery of the Hospital and its assets, which in pursuance of a royal order he was officially obliged to do, and for nothing, in their view he too had sold law. And so they prayed judgment.

Michael's rejoinder to this additional point in the charge[5] was to object that the two cases (Thorpe's and his own) were quite dissimilar. In Thorpe's case, he said, the parties were pleading before the chief justice as their judge, and in accordance with the laws of the land, circumstances in which a judge was bound not to take anything from the parties when doing them justice. In the present instance, no one had pleaded before him in his capacity as chancellor, and when he had been approached by the now master of the Hospital, bringing his papal bulls of provision, it was not as chancellor or judge, but rather as 'father and friend' of his son John; and, in any case, this was at a time when nobody knew whether or not John's application for a papal dispensation ('grace du Pape') had been successful. Besides, Michael continued, his counsel had discovered faults in the master's bulls, and it was for this reason that the master very willingly proffered the pension of £100, the fulfilment of this transaction being conditional upon Michael's abandoning his suit in the Curia on his son's behalf and refraining from challenging the defective bulls. The affair had not, therefore, been dealt with as a case brought before a judge, but rather settled, as could be proved by documentary evidence and by witnesses in the vill of Westminster, by amicable compromise ('par amyable composition'). Nor were the laws of England in question. And Michael did not see why, in these circumstances, he should be bound to answer to the party.

However, the judgment awarded[6] proved adverse in the event. This was hardly surprising, in view of the weighty reasons formally supporting it. Since the head of the Order of St Anthony was a known adherent of the anti-pope and also 'of the enmity of the king and power of France', (i.e. a French subject), the income of the Hospital should have gone to the Crown (a fact which ought to have been recognised at the start). Michael had admitted that what he had requested for his son was a hospital; and, having, when chancellor, sent to the Curia to procure the 'profit' for his son by papal collation of it as an ecclesiastical benefice, he had by this means deprived the king of its enjoyment. Nor had he denied receiving a revenue of 400 marks a year which was never restored to the king. Moreover, he had confessed to exacting a bargain from the present master of the Hospital as a papal provisor competing with his son, as a result of which, having in the meantime disregarded a direct royal order to deliver the 'profit', he had relinquished it only in return for the £100 annuity (with ample security for payment). Indeed, for anything that had so far been evinced, the 'profit' surely ought to have stayed in royal custody, at least until there had been discussion as to whether the Hospital was such a benefice as might lie in the papal gift or whether, by reason of the circumstances of the head of the Order, its income should appertain to the king. And then, finally, Michael had not satisfactorily answered the charge that he had not adequately informed the king of all this.

And the judgment awarded was that the revenues from the Hospital or procuracy from the time when granted until the present master took over, together with all the income from the £100 annuity from then until now, should be forfeit to the king, all leviable from Michael's own lands and goods and chattels. Also forfeited to the Crown were the monetary penalties contained in the covenants which the master had entered into with Michael and his son, as security for the payment of the annuity. But as far as the master's relations with Michael and his son were concerned, Michael was to be entirely discharged.

Although most of the extant chronicles of the period fully appreciated the significance of Michael's impeachment within the general context of events in the parliament of 1386, this fifth charge is the sole one to be given specific mention, and even then it occurs in only two extant works—the *Chronica Majora* of

Thomas Walsingham of St Albans[7] and the *Eulogium Historiarum* (an anonymous Canterbury chronicle).[8] It was no doubt because the charge involved an ecclesiastical institution and its assets, and also dealings with the papacy, that these writers' special interest was aroused. Even so, their actual references are extremely brief. Both chronicles, however, have the merit of indicating the chief source of the income of the English commandery of the Order of St Anthony of Vienne, which, for Michael and his son, was unquestionably the main attraction of the latter's proposed entry into the mastership of the London Hospital: what the *Eulogium* refers to simply as the 'collection' ('collecta') of St Anthony of Vienne, and Walsingham as 'the farm of all those pardoners ('quaestores') who are wont to go round with indulgences, collecting for the use of the fraternity of St Anthony' (for which privilege, Walsingham correctly adds, Michael was to pay the king twenty marks a year). This evidence confirms Michael's own testimony that the revenue of the Hospital was largely derived from pardons.

It is not known precisely when the Hospitallers of Vienne in Dauphiné, founded about 1100, formally constituted as an Order in 1231, and converted by Pope Boniface VIII in 1297 into one of Augustinian canons regular, established a hospice in England.[9] However, royal letters of protection were issued in 1219 to a 'procurator' and 'socii';[10] an additional patent, granted in 1225, conferred a licence to preach and to beg alms in this country;[11] and by 1243, when Henry III gave to the Order, for its use as a chapel, a converted synagogue on Broad Street in London,[12] the city was the centre of its English activities. Again in 1243 royal generosity went further, with the allowance of an annual Exchequer pension of twenty marks,[13] and in 1249 went further still, with a grant of the advowson of the church of All Saints, Hereford.[14] Even so, despite this royal assistance, the English commandery was never without its difficulties. The very frequency of royal letters of protection (albeit so constantly forthcoming as to suggest that they were virtually renewable on application) and, doubtless more significantly, occasional royal orders to arrest unauthorised persons fraudulently misappropriating alms (practices sometimes condemned by the papacy as well),[15] all point to this. A far more hazardous situation, however, had been created in the fourteenth century by Edward III's war with France. When the war began in 1337 the Order's English proctor-general[16] of the day was able to procure royal letters of protection for two years as being 'not of the power of the king of France';[17] but, naturally, there was now greater difficulty of access between England and Dauphiné, and the proctors ceased[18] either to attend general chapters at Vienne or to send annual payments. With the annexation of Dauphiné to the French crown in 1349, intercourse ceased altogether, and the position of the London Hospital became analogous to that of the alien priories generally. The renewal of proper relations permitted by the treaty of Brétigny-Calais (1360), including visits by the proctor, Geoffrey de Lymone, to general chapters in 1363 and 1366, lasted only as long as the peace (until 1369); by the outset of Richard II's reign a complete stoppage of monetary contributions by London to Vienne had supervened; and whatever links remained between the English commandery and the parent house were severed by the papal schism which began in 1378. Indeed, it may be safely presumed from the fact that when, on 8 May 1380, Geoffrey de Lymone was exempted from payment of all levies and contributions due from his preceptory to the Hospital at Vienne for the previous three years, it was by indult received from Clement VII at Avignon,[19] the proctor himself had left England and was a declared adherent of the anti-pope. In other words, his office as master of the London Hospital and preceptor of the English commandery was then vacant. And, whereas it was the 'schismacy' and 'enmity' of the head of the Order at Vienne which entitled the crown to the Order's English assets and income (as the charge against Michael de la Pole made clear), it was that vacancy which eventually afforded Michael the opportunity to intrude his son John.

It was on 20 October 1382, when Bishop Braybrook of London was chancellor, that, warranted by a writ of privy seal (as Michael pointed out at his trial), the grant of the custody of the Hospital and 'procuracy' of St Anthony in England was made to Michael and John together, for as long as it remained in the king's hands on account of the French war, and in return for an annual render to the Exchequer of twenty marks.[20] That the grant was a joint one was likely to have been less on account of John's youth and unfitness than because the fulfilment of a grant to him singly would ultimately have depended upon a papal provision to the mastership. John was certainly very young: when, in 1391, Urban VI's provision of him to a canonry at Beverley was disputed, it was part of the case against him that when the prebend had been conferred in 1385, he had been only about eleven years old,[21] meaning (if that was true) that at the time of the grant of St Anthony's to him and his father he was only about eight.[22] The question of John's fitness was, however, so far as we know, not raised at all at Michael's trial; and had Michael's suit in the Curia been successful, resulting in a papal provision to the mastership in his son's favour, the *royal* grant would doubtless have been converted into one to John alone. What, of course, was of immediate and real importance, apart from the basic charge of deception laid against Michael, was the loss of revenue to the Crown resulting from the grant: the fact that, in return for a comparatively minute rent, the De la Poles had been put in possession of a considerable income.

There is something of a conflict in the overall evidence relating to the amount of this income of the Hospital. Being dependent almost entirely on alms, it would most likely fluctuate very considerably. This appears, in fact, to have been the case: in 1391 the procuracy was believed at the Curia to be worth 200 marks a year;[23] in 1394, 600 marks;[24] and later on, in 1409 (and during the impoverishment of the Hospital under the mastership of John Macclesfield), no more than 150 marks.[25] However, so far as concerns the charge against Michael of depriving the Crown of revenue, that is substantiated by his own admission that the procuracy had turned out to be worth 400 marks a year, which was probably an average for the two years and more during which he and his son had benefited from their grant. If this, Michael's own, estimate was correct (and it is most unlikely to have been an overestimate), they must have enjoyed a total profit of not less than 855 marks,[26] a sum not all that short of the roughly 1,000 marks ('entour M marcz') mentioned in the initial charge. All that can be said in Michael's defence regarding this particular aspect of the charge—apart from his insistence that the king was fully informed of the discrepancy between the rent paid to the Exchequer and the income received, as well as of the charitable bestowal of his gains (a point seemingly never considered in his favour)—is that the annual rent of twenty marks demanded of him by the Exchequer was as much as was later required of his son's competitor for the mastership, who, moreover, soon obtained a reduction, partly on the ground that no previous preceptor had been so charged.[27] It must not, of course, be forgotten that the De la Poles, as a direct consequence of their interest in the London Hospital, stood to receive the considerable additional bonus deriving from their private arrangements with that rival competitor. And it may at once be said that the £100 annuity, which the latter had undertaken to pay the De la Poles, would itself have yielded, by the time of Michael's impeachment, about another 275 marks.[28]

John de la Pole's rival for the mastership of the Hospital remains anonymous throughout the official record of Michael's trial. He is there referred to only as 'le mestre q'ore est' or 'le provisour de St Antoyne' or, more simply, 'le provisour'. Unquestionably, however, he was Richard Brighouse, clerk; and some of the main facts connecting him with the offences laid to Michael's charge in this particular article of the impeachment are confirmed by evidence from the rolls of the Chancery. It was Richard Brighouse who, at Westminster on 17 December 1384, and along with John Brighouse and Henry Bubwith (the 'deux persones ovesqe lui' mentioned in the initial charge) entered into a bond with Michael, providing security for the payment of the annuity of £100 to him and his son John in survivorship,[29] the penalty for defeasance (leviable in Yorkshire) being 1,000 marks (*not*, unless there were other similar instruments neither enrolled in Chancery nor afterwords referred to in its records, the £3,000 mentioned in the charge). Then, on 9 January 1385, were issued, under the great seal, letters patent ratifying the estate that Richard Brighouse enjoyed in the English preceptory of the Order of St Anthony by virtue of letters apostolic;[30] and it was on the following day that the custody of the Hospital and its assets was committed to him for the duration of the war with France, and on condition of continuing to pay to the Exchequer the twenty marks rent.[31] The problem as to what prompted the annuity of £100 and the bond guaranteeing its payment—the question whether Richard Brighouse, in order to prevent his bulls of provision from being challenged, and possibly countermanded, at Rome, agreed with Michael to settle "out of Curia" and so granted the annuity and entered into the bond willingly, as Michael had alleged was the case, or whether, as the Commons insisted, the annuity and the bond were imposed on Brighouse as a condition of Michael's readiness, as chancellor, to accept a royal order to give him possession of the Hospital—the records do nothing to resolve. But certainly, whether willingly conceded or exacted under duress, the bond ensuring payment of the annuity preceded the commitment of the custody, and did so by barely three weeks, an interval suspiciously short, especially with the Christmas vacation coming in between. It looks as if the annuity and the bond were not so much a consequence as a cause, the cause or condition of the livery of the Hospital. And it was on this assumption that the Commons had referred to the case of Chief Justice Thorpe, charging Michael with having 'sold law'.

The judge in question was William de Thorpe, who, having been a royal judge since 1342, was promoted chief justice of the King's Bench in 1346.[32] The facts of the case referred to are soon told: Thorpe was charged with malversation in 1350 and, after commissioners had been authorised, by a writ of 3 November that year, to examine him and proceed to judgment, he confessed to having received, from five men indicted before him, bribes amounting in all to £100, in return for which he had caused writs of exigent against them to be stayed; at first committed to the Tower and subjected to forfeiture of lands and goods, following the issue of another writ on 19 November he was sentenced to be degraded and hanged; however, the capital sentence was immediately commuted to one of imprisonment, and in the following year the king pardoned him, although, in the meantime, on the advice of the Lords in the parliament of February 1351,[33] the judgment at first pronounced had been confirmed as reasonable, on the ground that Thorpe had admitted receiving gifts, knowing this to be a breach of his official oath and when fully aware of the condign punishment.

Michael's submission regarding the charge of having 'sold law' like Chief Justice Thorpe—that the cases were not comparable—was unsuccessful. Admittedly, the judgment makes no further reference to Thorpe's case. But the Commons' rejection of Michael's explanation—that the annuity and bond were the outcome of private arrangement voluntarily entered into by Richard Brighouse—clearly prevailed: fulfilment of the royal order to deliver the Hospital to Brighouse ought not to have been dependent upon such a 'bargain', and the allegation that there was no connexion, that the one was not a cause or condition of the other, was a mere pretence or subterfuge. Not only had Michael farmed the procuracy for a grotesquely inadequate return to the Crown, but had exacted a large annual pension from Brighouse before handing over the Hospital. And so, under the judgment, not only the financial gain made by the De la Poles from the procuracy, but also the yield from the annuity, were to be forfeited. And, of course, the annuity itself was to lapse. The Commons had all the facts on their side regarding this aspect of the charge, and were able to substantiate their accusation. This was, basically, that a royal official, especially one so highly placed as the chancellor, had no business to act, indeed could not properly act, in his private capacity in a matter involving the Crown.

But it was not only the ex-chancellor who suffered financial loss. For, although the annuity Brighouse had contracted to pay the De la Poles had been annulled, the bond guaranteeing payment had evidently not. The parliamentary judgment, in fact, by declaring the bond forfeit to the Crown, assumed its continued efficacy; and, now that the bond had plainly been contravened by the discontinuance of payment of the annuity, the forfeit or penal sanction the bond contained was regarded as *ipso facto* enforceable, with the result that all that would, in the ordinary course of events, have accrued to the De la Poles automatically became a debt owed to the king. Neither Richard Brighouse nor his successor as master of St Anthony's escaped the consequences of the former's involvement in the affair. Not even the Hospital as an institution did so. The Hospital was taken into the king's hands pending recovery, from Brighouse and his erstwhile mainpernors, of the 1,000 marks forfeit under the bond, and it was apparently not until 20 May 1389 that arrangements could be made for the king's financial satisfaction, viz. payment to the Exchequer of £40 in hand, and of £40 a year until all arrears had been met. Only then was Brighouse restored to the custody.[34] And although, after Brighouse's death before 24 November that same year (when John Macclesfield, a clerk of the privy seal, was presented by the king for institution as preceptor),[35] a royal order was immediately issued for the seizure of Brighouse's goods and chattels with a view to obtaining more of what was still outstanding of the debt,[36] the residue remained as a charge upon the income of the Hospital between then and 27 March 1391, this being the date of a royal pardon and discharge granted to Macclesfield and his successors in the mastership.[37]

Notes

1 *Rot. Parl.*, III, 216a.
2 Vienne (Dauphiné) was in the obedience of the anti-pope, Clement VII, which fact made the head of the Order a schismatic (see p. 177). England adhered, of course, to the 'true' pope, Urban VI.
3 Ibid., 217b.
4 Ibid., 218a, 218b. Regarding Chief Justice Thorpe, see pp. 180–1.
5 Ibid., 219a.

6 Ibid., 220a.
7 Thomas Walsingham, *Historia Anglicana*, ed. H. T. Riley (R.S., 1863–4), II, 149.
8 *Eulogium Historiarum*, ed. F. S. Haydon (R.S., 1858–63), III, 360.
9 Rose Graham, 'The Order of St Antonie de Viennois and its English Commandery, St Anthony's, Threadneedle Street' *Archaeological Journal*, LXXXIV (1927), 341–406. Miss Graham's quite full account is slightly flawed as a result of her unawareness of the mention of the London Hospital in Michael's impeachment, an omission which led her to assume that the income of the Hospital was 'extremely small' (op. cit., 358).
10 *CPR*, *1216–25*, 201.
11 Graham, op. cit., 349.
12 Ibid., 350.
13 *CPR*, *1232–47*, 381.
14 *C. Charter R.*, *1226–57*, 345.
15 E.g. *CPR*, *1266–72*, 171; ibid., *1327–30*, 23, 114; Graham, op. cit., 355.
16 The head of the English commandery was known by this title in 1273 (*CPR*, *1292–1301*, 138), but he came in the fourteenth century to be called more usually either preceptor or master, sometimes keeper, of the Hospital, i.e. the London Hospital.
17 *CPR*, *1334–38*, 500.
18 Graham, 356.
19 *Calendar of Papal Registers, Papal Letters, 1362–1404*, 240.
20 *CFR*, *1377–83*, 324.
21 *Calendar of Papal Registers, Petitions, 1342–1419*, 409.
22 John's boyhood had not, however, prevented Urban VI from providing him to a cathedral canonry at York in March 1381, expressly in consideration of the losses his father had undergone as a result of his imprisonment in Germany (*CPR*, *1377–81*, 610). Nor was it to stand in the way of his being allowed by a papal dispensation of 1383–4 to be tonsured, and to receive minor orders and hold a benefice without cure, even a cathedral prebend (*Papal Letters*, *1396–1404*, 208). Regarding John's youthfulness, it is important to bear in mind that the mastership of the London Hospital and procuracy was, in canonical terms, neither a dignity or 'personatus', nor conventual or elective (*Papal Letters*, *1362–1404*, 419; ibid., *1404–15*, 162).
23 *Papal Letters*, *1362–1404*, 419.
24 Ibid., 254.
25 Ibid., *1404–15*, 162; *1417–31*, 374.

26 400 m × 2¼ (years) = 900 m, *minus* 20 m (rent payable to the Exchequer) × 2¼ (years) = 45 m: 855 m.

27 On the ground that the London Hospital of St Anthony's had no lands, only alms, and that no previous preceptor had been so charged, the rent arranged in the grant of 10 January 1385 was reduced by £5 on 5 June following, with the ultimate prospect of total remission (*CPR, 1381–85*, 582).

28 The annuity of £100 (150 marks) would then have been owing for twenty-two months (December 1384–October 1386).

29 *CCR, 1381–85*, 593; *CFR, 1383–91*, 289; *CPR, 1388–92*, 389.

30 *CPR, 1381–85*, 528.

31 *CFR, 1383–91*, 84.

32 *D.N.B.*, *sub nomine*, XIX, 804.

33 *Rot. Parl.*, II, 227b. Thorpe, although not restored to his office of chief justice, was made second baron of the Exchequer on 24 May 1352, and sat among the judges in parliament in 1354 and 1355 (ibid., 254, 267).

34 *CFR, 1383–91*, 289. Brighouse and two different mainpernors were now jointly bound to the king in a sum of £80, forfeitable in the event of failure to pay the new farm rent within a month of any term.

35 *CPR, 1388–92*, 164. Following an order of Boniface IX to the collector for the Apostolic Chamber in England, dated 17 December 1389, to collate John Macclesfield to the preceptory after he should have worn the Augustinian habit for three months (*Papal Letters, 1362–1404*, 419), Macclesfield was in possession of the Hospital by 6 February 1390 when given royal letters of protection for a year (*CPR, 1388–92*, 214); and although papal orders to collate a new provisor were issued on 22 August 1391, on the grounds that Macclesfield had neither assumed the habit nor been admitted by the papal collector (*Papal Letters*, loc. cit.), he remained in possession, and on 15 June 1392 Boniface conferred the Hospital upon him in *commendam* for ten years (ibid., 430). The nomination, by the high master of the Order, of a canon of the mother house of Vienne in 1409, although supported by Pope Alexander V (the new Conciliar pope to whom England adhered), had no effect; and Macclesfield continued as master of St Anthony's, London, until 1423, when, apparently, he died (Graham, op. cit., 361).

36 *CPR, 1388–92*, 208.

37 Ibid., 389.

Conclusion

The accusations made in parliament against Michael de la Pole in 1386 deserve no more to be "written down", still less to be "written off", than does the trial itself, of which the immediate political consequences and prospective constitutional significance have always been regarded as important. Naturally, closer attention has been paid by historians to these latter aspects than to the actual charges preferred. But the charges themselves, even though some differed from others as much in outcome as in character, drew attention to matters considered at the time to be of serious concern. And it is to misunderstand their relevance to current problems to regard them as 'frivolous', 'trivial' or 'paltry'. Such contemptuously dismissive terms are inappropriate.

That the charges were far from frivolous, trivial or paltry may be confidently asserted no less of the four (articles 2, 3, 6 and 7) against which Michael did, on the whole, successfully defend himself, or concerning which the Lords imposed no personal penalty, than of the other three (articles 1, 4 and 5) upon which the Lords found against, and penalised, him. All the *four* bore upon Michael's alleged negligence or remissness in the discharge of his official duties as chancellor in relation to issues of public concern: sins of omission. Of those four, the sixth might seem at first sight to have been of no great importance. Admittedly, it related to royal pardons for felonies (including treasons) which, it was implied in Michael's defence, the Commons believed to have been authorised by insufficient warrants. But, for all immediate practical purposes, its chief concern was with a grant of franchises extending the jurisdictional powers of the constable of Dover castle; and this, despite the Commons' exaggerated complaint that the grant had been 'to the disherison of the Crown and to the subversion of all royal courts and of the law', was essentially of local interest. Moreover, as Michael himself said, the grant could easily be annulled (as, in fact, the Lords were to demand, and was soon to be done). In any case, the problem of the constable's jurisdiction was one that was to remain as persistently troublesome after 1386 as it had been from long before, and it was a problem evidently difficult to solve. Great provocation had been offered by the timing of the grant of the charter, and by the unfortunate identity of the immediate beneficiary (the grant was made when Michael was under imminent threat of dismissal and impeachment, and in favour of Sir Simon de Burley, another of the king's closest friends). But, provocation apart, that the charge about the Dover charter was not at all frivolous is made clear not only by Michael's own admission that the charter had been allowed to pass the great seal 'lightly' and ill-advisedly, but also, and more significantly, by the fact that, when the charter was cancelled, it was recorded that this was because it had been issued 'irregularly'. Quite simply, the charter had been warranted by signet letter alone. Objection to this 'irregularity' was, indeed, at the bottom of the charge taken as a whole: it applied also, if only similarly by implication, to that part of the charge that related to pardons, for signet letters, especially in Michael's last year of office, had been taking the place of privy seal writs as direct warrants for letters of pardon issued under the great seal, as well as for other sorts of Chancery instruments. And, certainly, this was no trivial matter. It raised the whole deep-seated, constitutional question as to the means by which was to be restrained or controlled the exercise of the king's own personal prerogative.

Quite important though the sixth charge was, all the remaining three (articles 2, 3 and 7) of the four which raised the question of Michael's negligent discharge of his duty as chancellor were of an even more serious order. Certainly they were from parliament's own proper point of view. For, here, the Commons were alleging that Michael had violated, or at least left unfulfilled, certain decisions reached in the last previous parliament, the parliament of 1385: decisions bearing upon the system and conduct of royal finance and, where appropriations of taxes voted by that parliament were involved, upon the overseas policy of the government and the defence of the realm. The three had this in common, too: in each case Michael's defence rested upon the plea that he was not alone accountable, and that, if blame did lie, his fellow ministers and other members of the royal Council must share it, a plea which the Lords were to accept.

The first of these three charges (article 2) referred to an ordinance of the parliament of 1385 which, following an investigation by a parliamentary committee of nine lords, set out ample ways and means of increasing royal revenue and reducing expenditure, an ordinance which Michael had undertaken to execute, doing so openly in parliament, and thus assuming a distinctly personal responsibility. In defending himself against the charge proper, he was able to point to the achievement of some economies. But although these were far from negligible, at least at Brest and Cherbourg (as record evidence confirms), they represented only a partial retrench-ment; and, in any case, Michael said nothing on the score of increasing royal income. His actions had evidently stopped well short of what the ordinance had prescribed, and, this being the case, it must be said that his defence was hardly satisfactory enough.

The second of the three charges (article 3) in which the Commons complained of Michael's non-observance of deci-sions taken by the 1385 parliament involved the question of appropriation of taxes, with particular reference to provision for the safe-keeping of the seas, which, in view of the likely renewal of the threat of French invasion in the following year, was a vital aspect of national defence. Given that the parliament had granted in direct taxation no more than one and a half tenths and fifteenths, and had appropriated this grant to the support of John of Gaunt's expedition to Spain, help for Ghent, the defence of the Scottish March, and the protection of maritime traffic and defence of the coasts, it must soon have become doubtful whether these appropriations could all be adequately complied with. The incumbent liabilities were too many and, taken together, too expensive. Confusion was bound to result, possibly aggravated by the adulteration, by parliament itself, of the Commons' original scheme for implementing the appropriations, i.e. by entrusting expenditure of the subsidy to special 'treasurers of war' alone (not that such a scheme, if past experience was anything to go by, was sure of success). Regarding the keeping of the seas, provision of shipping for this purpose was certain to run the government into difficulties in the year following the meeting of the parliament, for all the objects of appropriation (even, to some extent, defence against the Scots) depended directly upon the available supply of ships, and this would in turn depend upon the number and timing of the calls made upon it. So far as this question is concerned, the policies represented by the appropriations conflicted with one another, and, even when, almost immediately, the need to help the Gantois ceased to be a problem, what had still to be arranged remained a source of confusion. For this, the parliament of 1385, too sanguine as to what was feasible, must take the blame: not the Council, still less the chancellor alone. Michael had evidently drawn hostile attention to himself by the very personal part he had played in the aftermath of the seizure of the Genoese convoy by naval forces; but, whether or not he was impeached of this, the charge that he had so neglected to carry out the tax appropriations of 1385 as to jeopardise the safe-keeping of the sea would seem to have been the least reasonable of all the charges preferred against him.

The charge of negligence on Michael's part contained in the seventh charge was of a no less serious kind, being on the score of his alleged responsibility for the government's failure to prevent the loss of Ghent to the French. Admittedly, following an ordinance of the parliament of 1385 authorising the financing by loan of an English expeditionary force for the relief of the town, Michael had acted as promptly as was reasonably possible after the dissolution of the parliament, recruiting a force, taking steps to send it to Flanders, and raising the loan with which to pay for it. But this force, being so small that, when it could no longer be used as first intended, it was made to serve merely as a reinforcement to the garrison at Berwick-upon-Tweed, would hardly have afforded adequate support to the Gantois. In any case, Michael's measures came too late: the start of the final negotiations at Tournai, where surrender was imposed upon Ghent and the rest of Flanders, precisely coincided with the dissolution of the parliament and with the first steps Michael then took to fulfil parliament's intentions. Given, however, that he acted as soon as was reasonably possible after the dissolution (and perhaps he was not even entitled to act before then), it may well be that the charge was in reality levelled against him partly on account of his whole long-standing attitude to the problem of Flanders, partly, and more especially, because, earlier in 1385, he had been a willing party to the adoption of a policy which, in its effects, was destined to help make the collapse of Ghent a near certainty. In 1385 English military assistance had, in fact, been urgently needed by the Gantois most of all in the summer, when, having captured the port of Damme on 15 July, they had lost it to the French on 24 August, after a six weeks' siege. Had an English expedition been sent, the siege must have lasted longer, indeed might possibly have failed; and, in view of French preparations at nearby Sluis for a great seaborne invasion of England, such a scheme would have seemed as justifiable from the English standpoint as beneficial to the Gantois. It was, however, left to the latter to ensure, by holding out in Damme so long as they did, the abandonment of the invasion. Any English relief of the siege had, in fact, been ruled out by a decision taken by the English government at least six weeks before the Gantois even first captured the port, the decision, that is, to commit a very large English army to an expedition into Scotland which, long delayed, happened to coincide with the siege. But not only must it have then seemed that the English government had turned its back on Flanders: with the Scottish expedition led by Richard II in person and accompanied by his chief ministers (including the chancellor, the treasurer, and the keeper of the privy seal), his court, and many of the great nobles (including his three uncles), any revival of interest in the cause of Ghent would have depended upon the king's return south, and also upon decisions requiring the sanction and support of a parliament. The Scottish expedition having proved a wasted effort, indeed a fiasco, it was not until 3 September that, with the king back at Westminster, parliament was summoned. But although the situation of Ghent was now parlous in the extreme, it was evidently agreed that parliament need not meet until 20 October. Such an interval between summons and assembly was not unusually long, but taking into account also the time it would take parliament to reach any decision on the Flemish question, it was too long in the circumstances. Admittedly, when parliament met, negotiations between Ghent and Philip of Burgundy and his French allies were yet to begin; however, they did so soon afterwards, and by the time parliament had decided upon helping the Gantois, the possibility of even obstructing a surrender, let alone preventing it, was virtually non-existent. The Commons, in venting their chagrin in 1386 at the government's unsuccessful gamble on Ghent's capacity to continue to resist throughout the second half of 1385 and beyond, by putting the blame on Michael, were doubtless not only appreciating the great influence in the Council and in parliament given him by his office, but were also recalling the fact that he had never been in favour of an all-out effort to sustain the Flemish rebellion, indeed had sometimes openly revealed his distaste for such a policy. Michael's almost frenetic haste in taking steps to help the Gantois at the end, but when it was too late, would seem to have been in part designed to save face; indeed, the measures that were taken almost amounted to a "cover-up", an attempt to gloss over his previous attitude to the 'voie de Flandres'. And it is to be doubted whether the

Lords, in excusing Michael's personal responsibility for the failure of parliament's attempt to secure the relief of Ghent in the autumn of 1385, were being quite fair to his accusers, the Commons.

The other three charges (articles 1, 4 and 5) of the seven brought against Michael were, basically, all on the score of peculation: deliberate exploitation of the office of chancellor for his own private gain, conduct resulting in financial loss to the Crown. Sins of commission, therefore. In all three charges, it was alleged by the Commons that, when soliciting and accepting certain grants from the king, Michael had practised deception; and in one charge (article 1) explicitly, and in the other two (articles 4 and 5) implicitly, that he had broken his oath as either councillor or chancellor to secure the king's advantage in all respects, including the financial. Regarding the charge of deception, Michael consistently emphasised that, whenever there was doubt about the propriety of a grant or the precise form it should take, he had made the king fully aware of any disadvantage to the Crown, only for his advice to be rejected; and regarding the charge of perjury, he ridiculed it as nonsensical on the ground that the oath, if so literally interpreted, would have prevented grants in anybody's favour, let alone his own. The Commons' insinuation that the grants and concessions he had received went beyond his deserts was to some extent rebutted by Lord Scrope's testimony to his career in the royal service under both Edward III and Richard II. But the Commons' charge that those grants and concessions, whether received before or after his promotion to his earldom, were excessive in other ways, was well sustained, and is amply borne out by extra-parliamentary record evidence, evidence available in the records of the Chancery itself, most of it dating from the time of Michael's custody of the great seal.

One must admit that some of Michael's grants called into question at his trial preceded his appointment as chancellor (March 1383). This was so in the case of the annuity of 400 marks, an annuity which, charged on the Hull customs, he had inherited from his father in 1366: it was in May 1382 that

Michael was allowed to exchange a little over half of it (220 marks) for lands that had recently escheated on the death of William of Ufford, earl of Suffolk. But what he had not scrupled to do when chancellor was to confirm this part-exchange (July 1383) and then to arrange for the conversion of the remainder of the annuity (180 marks), first into a grant in reversion of other Ufford land (August 1384) and, pending this event, into a grant of equivalent income from equally safe sources of royal revenue, fee-farms and, again, land (November 1385). It was also before he became chancellor that, in October 1382, Michael and his son John were granted the 'procuracy' of the Order of St Anthony of Vienne in England, at so absurdly low an annual rental (twenty marks) as to have yielded them, over the period of their enjoyment of the grant, an inordinately great profit (not grossly overestimated, in the Commons' figure, at 1,000 marks), which ought all to have gone to the Crown. But it was when Michael was chancellor that, in December 1384, he successfully concluded a compromise with his son's competitor for the mastership of the London Hospital of the Order, a private settlement which brought him and his son, in survivorship, an annuity of £100, its payment guaranteed by a recognisance for 1,000 marks. It was similarly when he was chancellor that Michael had successfully concluded his previously unsatisfactory dealings over the annuity of £50 which, charged on the Hull customs, he had obtained in Edward III's reign from Tidemann of Limburg, in return for the cancellation of a personal debt of 1,000 marks. Ignoring any question of Tidemann's legal right to have retained the annuity (which was in doubt), Michael first, on 15 May 1385, regularised the transfer by obtaining a royal pardon and a fresh grant to himself; then, on 20 August following, he exchanged two thirds of the annuity for two thirds of the manor of Faxfleet and a supplementary rent; and shortly afterwards, on 3 September, he obtained, in anticipation of the whole manor becoming available, an out-and-out grant of it, up to the full value of the annuity. What, in effect, he had contrived was to have created an income for himself where none had previously existed.

What, of course, had in the Commons' view made the exchanges so outrageous was that the annuities in question (the inherited annuity of 400 marks and the transferred annuity of £50) had been exchanged, either for land, or for income in large part deriving from land. And what, too, the Commons had clearly recognised was that the calculations upon which the exchanges had been based were too simply arithmetical, and took no account of circumstantial realities. No proper comparison, they felt, could be made between a royal grant of income from customs levied on exported wool and one of income from largely landed estate: the former, depending upon the exigencies of the trade, the prosperity of the port designated, and the competing claims of royal annuitants and creditors upon the revenue collected there, yielded only uncertain expectations; whereas landed estate was replete with assurance of regular income. But not only that: a grant of land tended to be relatively even more reliable, given that the underlying assessment of its value by the Exchequer would itself be based upon extents which, whether old or new, were only too likely to be unrealistic, erring on the side of undervaluation. And when the Commons attacked Michael (as in articles 1 and 4) for having accepted lands that were undervalued, they were also well aware that, when a grant of landed estate involved a number of contributory parcels, the lower their valuations were, the more would extra lands, or else additional income from other sources, inevitably be required to make up the total sum of the grant.

It was for all these different reasons that most of Michael's grants involving land attracted the hostile attention of the Commons. Justifiably so, and not least as regards the question of undervaluation. Despite Michael's denial, undervaluation in some measure certainly occurred in the case of the exchange of the annuity of £50 (once Tidemann of Limburg's) for the manor of Faxfleet. Nor can there be much doubt but that it also occurred in the case of those escheated Ufford lands for which he exchanged his inherited annuity of 400 marks, over half of it, in 1382, for immediate possession, and the rest, in 1384, in reversion; and in the case, too, of those additional Ufford lands which, designed eventually to yield all the £500 a year he was given when promoted earl in 1385, he then acquired only in reversion, the prompt specification of which lands, however, made either fresh extents or acceptance of existing valuations an essential prerequisite. There may be no reason to doubt that, so far as this particular grant is concerned, Michael had offered to accept fresh extents, instead of the valuations made on the death of William of Ufford in 1382 (on the basis of which the lands were currently held by William's widow and the queen), or that he had only had recourse to those already available valuations because the king insisted. But if, when Michael said (as say he did) that these were 'the highest', he meant the highest of all previous valuations, he was in error; and if he meant the highest possible, he was merely being disingenuous, for, obviously, he could have had no idea what would be the result of extents that were still to be made. Moreover, it might be argued that in case fresh valuations proved higher, more advantageous to the Crown in the circumstances, the king ought to have been advised not to be so indulgent. In any case, the transaction had evidently been contrived in haste, and hurried through; and although, with this particular grant of Ufford lands remaining reversionary, actual possession was not of course in question, it was to Michael's advantage at least to know precisely what he, or his heirs, would obtain in future. (And he might be able, in the meantime, to convert one or more of these lands held only in reversion into a lease, as he had soon done with Costessey, granted him in reversion in 1384.)

That the Commons' charges of peculation against Michael were well enough argued completely to satisfy the Lords is obvious from the latter's judgments, which were all condemnatory. What the Lords considered proved was that Michael had exploited his high public office for private profit, in all respects to the loss of the Crown, and in one charge (concerning the mastership of the Hospital of St Anthony's) to the disadvantage of one of the king's subjects as well. Whatever deficiencies in the evidence relating to any one of the particular charges falling into this category, and however energetic Michael's defence to them all, those charges so supported one another, in the sense that their general drift was much the same, as to become a coherent whole, something more than just the sum of its parts. At the very least, the Lords must have felt, there was too much smoke for there not to have been some fire. And they reacted accordingly: the Lords' adverse judgments on the several articles in question were greatly to Michael's detriment. In fact, all the lands Michael had received, whether in exchange for annuities, or as endowment of his comital status, were to be resumed for the Crown, all the income which the lands had yielded in the meantime being also forfeit. Moreover, the sum of 1,000 marks which, as Michael had alleged, had been paid for one of the exchanges was to remain in the king's hands, as part payment of the additional 'fine and ransom' he was to pay before being released from prison. And although, in the case of St Anthony's Hospital, the Lords only implicitly rejected Michael's denial that he (like Chief Justice Thorpe) had 'sold law', and ruled out all further litigation on the part of the new master of the Hospital, they insisted on forfeiture of the total income which he and his son had derived from their bargain, as well as of the recognisance guaranteeing its fulfilment.

What, in these charges of a personal character, the Commons had complained of, and the Lords, in their judicial decisions, felt obliged to insist upon, was first that, in a time of financial difficulty of abnormal proportions for the government, the major officials of the Crown bore a heavy responsibility for ensuring that particularly their own rewards for service were kept within decent limits, and second that exploitation of public office for private gain was a punishable offence. In parliament's judgment, Michael had flagrantly misused his custody of the great seal for his own ends. The lesson seems not to have been lost upon, at any rate, his immediate successor as chancellor, Thomas Arundel, then bishop of Ely: on 20 November 1387, the very day on which, by letters close under the great seal, the Exchequer was ordered to make to Thomas, as bishop of Ely, allowances of certain liberties and profits granted by ancient charters to his predecessors in the see, he temporarily surrendered the seal, presumably to avoid any suspicion of self-interest or partiality.[1] Arundel's own successor, William of Wykeham (chancellor in 1389–91), was to be nothing like so punctilious, certainly not in the last half-year of his tenure of office. During that period Wykeham allowed to pass the great seal numerous licences for the alienation in mortmain, to his own scholastic foundations (the collegiate school at Winchester and New College, Oxford), of many English manors and lands once belonging to French monasteries, all these manors and lands being then made quit of the fee-farm rents owed to the Crown.[2] No other chancellor in the last years of Richard II's reign or under Henry IV, however, followed Wykeham's example until, on 10 March 1409, Thomas Arundel, now in his fourth term of office as chancellor, was granted, for life and free of all charges, the castle and lordship of Queenborough (Kent). But how preoccupied by the need for caution Arundel again was is clearly demonstrated by the fact that, on this occasion too, he temporarily surrendered the great seal to the king, so that the letters close making the grant could be sealed in his absence.[3]

Notes

1   *CCR, 1385–89*, 362–3, 459.
2   *CPR, 1389–91*, 417–18, 433.
3   *CCR, 1405–9*, 498.

Epilogue

Our subject being the impeachment of Michael de la Pole in 1386, his later career, which although eventful was to be short, may be dealt with at no great length. Losing possession of such of the lands as he had held by royal grant and had, of course, forfeited in accordance with the judgements of the 'Wonderful Parliament', Michael was expressly allowed to retain his title of earl of Suffolk (and the usual annuity of £20 charged on the issues of that county).[1] Moreover, although he was sentenced by the Lords to be imprisoned, pending payment of fine and ransom for his various 'defautes et mesprisions',[2] and apparently ordered by parliament to be sent to Corfe castle,[3] neither penalty was enforced without modification. Indeed, both penalties were soon remitted by the king, and by Christmas (four weeks after parliament's dissolution) not only was Michael accommodated on the king's orders at Windsor, but he then and there, and with every mark of royal favour shown him, joined in the court's festivities. During 1387, constantly on the move in close attendance upon the king, he remained foremost among his advisers. In August, according to the chronicler Knighton, he was a prime mover of the repudiation of the conduct and acts of the 'Wonderful Parliament' represented by the Questions put to the royal judges at Shrewsbury and Nottingham, on which latter occasion, Knighton says[4], he threatened Chief Justice Bealknap with death if he did not seal the document; and, on the evidence of the document itself, he was one of its witnesses. On 28 October the king sent him (with Archbishop Neville) to enquire as to the loyalty of London,[5]

and on 10 November Michael accompanied Richard at his entry
into the city and return to Westminster.[6] It was in the following
week that, in fear of the implacable hostility of the king and his
friends, as evinced by the Questions put to the judges, and
aware of the expiry on 20 November of the lawful term of the
parliamentary commission set up in 1386, the opposition
lords—the duke of Gloucester and the earls of Arundel and
Warwick—gathered their forces at Harringay (Middlesex),
bent upon a "showdown". According to the chronicler
Walsingham,[7] Michael now did his utmost to prevent attempts
to reconcile the king and Gloucester, only to be reminded of his
own condemnation in the 'Wonderful Parliament' by Bishop
Braybrooke of London, who told him to keep quiet. And, in
fact, at Waltham Cross (Essex) on 14 November, Gloucester
and the two earls were met by a delegation of members of the
parliamentary commission bent on appeasement.[8] What then
transpired was an acceptance by the three lords of an invitation
from the king to meet him at Westminster, this accompanied,
however, by a formal Appeal (*accusatio*) lodged against five of
the king's foremost friends—Archbishop Neville, Robert de
Vere, duke of Ireland, Chief Justice Tresilian, Sir Nicholas
Brembre and, of course, De la Pole—coupled with a demand
for their arrest. When, on 17 November in Westminster Hall,
the three appellants duly appeared, the king was forced to
accept their demands, promising that the appellees should be
tried for high treason in the next parliament, and that
parliament should meet on 3 February 1388.[9] De Vere's
attempt to support the king with an army raised in Cheshire,
Lancashire and Wales failed disastrously at Radcot Bridge on
20 December, by when the original three appellants had been
joined by Henry of Bolingbroke, earl of Derby, and Thomas
Mowbray, earl of Nottingham; and it was now all five who, on
the 27th, renewed the appeal, which then assumed its final
form.[10] It contained no accusations against De la Pole alone,
but he was associated with the other appellees in all but a very
few of its thirty-nine articles, the gist of the most important
charges being that, taking advantage of the king's youth, they

had monopolised his confidence, estranged him from the magnates, 'accroached' to themselves (appropriated) royal power, enriched themselves at the expense of the Crown, impugned the parliamentary commission of 1386–7 and to that end suborned the judges, and plotted (even with the French) against the lives of the appellants, so encouraging civil war. Whatever may be said of Michael's fellow members of the cabal, of Michael himself it may safely be said that, having been taught a lesson in 1386, he had shown in 1387 that he had failed to learn it.

After exception had been taken to the parliamentary writs of summons first issued on 17 December, on the ground that they had broken with custom in requiring that the knights of the shire to be elected should have been quite neutral in recent disputes ('in debatis modernis magis indifferentes'), fresh writs excluding that offensive *clausula* were issued on 1 January 1388;[11] and the sheriffs were also ordered to take steps to ensure the appearance of the appellees in parliament. To a large extent, of course, that order was already impossible of fulfilment. Robert de Vere, following upon his escape from Radcot Bridge on 20 December, and after a brief interview with the king in London, had gone down to Queenborough and sailed for Holland.[12] Archbishop Neville, however, as Knighton says,[13] had fled northwards as early as 20 November. And, to begin with, De la Pole can hardly have dallied much longer: a first escape to Calais, where his brother Edmund was captain of the castle, availed him nothing, for Sir William Beauchamp, the governor of the town, sent him back to the king in London;[14] and it was no later than 20 December (the date of Radcot Bridge) that a royal serjeant was sent to arrest him at Hull,[15] where he had gone by the king's leave and from where, presumably, he finally made good his escape, this time to Dordrecht, ultimately to Paris. Further orders for his arrest, issued on 27 December and 4 January,[16] were to prove equally abortive.

When parliament met as promised on Monday, 3 February 1388, of all the appellees only Brembre was in custody and able to answer to the charges of the Lords Appellant. The latter were ready to prosecute their appeal immediately;[17] and when, on the opening day of the session, proclamation was made in Westminster Hall, and at the great door of the Palace, formally requiring the appearance of the absent appellees, the appellants requested that their default should be recorded and judgment passed. Legal advice having been given on the Tuesday that, because it was high treason that was at issue, the appeal was for the Lords to judge, and by no other law than 'the law and course of Parliament', the Lords Appellant repeated their request; and on the Wednesday, the day when the Lords Spiritual protested their inability under the canon law to be party to any judgment, they did so again, and also demanded Brembre's appearance. The Lords Temporal, having then spent a week of 'grant labour et diligence' in examining the articles of the appeal and receiving evidence, on the 13th found all the absentees charged 'coupables notoriement', each on every article touching him; and, 'come Juges de Parlement en cest cas', they adjudged them guilty and convicted of treason, sentencing them to be drawn and hanged as traitors and enemies of the king and kingdom, and declared that they and their heirs should be disinherited, and their lands and goods and chattels forfeited (and in the case of Archbishop Neville that the temporalities of his see should be seized into the king's hands). It was now a foregone conclusion that Brembre would be similarly convicted and sentenced. And so it was: arraigned on 17 February, he was condemned on the 20th and hanged the same day, the day after Tresilian was arrested and, as having been previously convicted, hanged without more ado.[18]

Michael de la Pole and the other two appellees (Neville and De Vere), all of whom had now fled the realm, did of course, and likewise their heirs, suffer the remaining penalty imposed by the Lords Temporal on 13 February 1388, i.e. the forfeiture of lands and personalty, which was carried out forthwith.[19] In the case of De la Pole's eldest son, Sir Michael, some slight mitigation of the effects of the forfeiture was, however, obtained on 23 March following (within days of the end of the first session of the 'Merciless Parliament'): at the petition of the earl of Warwick and certain other lords, 'cosyns et alliez' of Sir

Michael's wife, Katherine, a daughter of Hugh, late earl of Stafford, and Warwick's own niece, the king then granted the couple the manors of Harpswell and Blyborough (Lincolnshire) and Grassthorpe (Nottinghamshire), De la Pole manors settled on them as jointure by the earl of Suffolk long before his forfeiture but seized, nonetheless, into the king's hands.[20] However, the three manors, then thought to be worth £100 a year, proved not to be so, and Sir Michael and his wife were driven to petition in the parliament of January 1390 that such other lands might be granted as would raise the income to the level intended.[21] Moreover, although the forfeitures awarded in the 'Merciless Parliament' were never meant to apply to entailed estates, it was only after his father's death that Sir Michael was allowed possession of lands of this sort (in Norfolk and Suffolk on 3 December 1389, in Yorkshire on 3 February 1390, and in the palatinate of Durham on 1 February 1392).[22] And although in January 1393, not long after Robert de Vere's death, the title of earl of Oxford was revived in favour of his uncle, Aubrey de Vere, no such restoration of the Suffolk title took place until 28 January 1398. Then, during the Shrewsbury session of Richard II's last parliament, the proceedings of the 'Merciless Parliament' were totally annulled and, accordingly, Sir Michael was restored to his father's dignities, obtaining, on 19 June following, a patent conferring the earldom, with remainder to his male heirs in the direct line, whom failing, those of his father. An immediate consequence of the 'revolution' of 1399 was a repeal in Henry IV's first parliament of the acts of Richard II's last, involving of course a confirmation of the proceedings of 1388, so that Sir Michael, once again falling under his father's attainder, forfeited all his honours. A very temporary reverse, however: not only did he then obtain restitution of most of his inheritance, but on 15 November 1399, 'in consideration of his services after the king's advent', was restored as earl of Suffolk, on terms similar to those of 1398.[23]

The three appellees who survived the 'Merciless Parliament' were fated to live out their days in exile. Any idea that they might sometime be pardoned, rehabilitated at law, and allowed to return to England, had been quite ruled out when, before the end of the parliament, the Commons petitioned that such a proposal should result in a charge of treason, a petition with which the king had no option but to concur.[24] Nor, in this respect, did Richard's dramatic resumption of personal powers of government, in May 1389, make any difference. So far as the former earl of Suffolk was concerned, time hardly permitted; he died only four months later (on 5 September, at Paris).[25] Not that that mattered, in the sense that he might have died inopportunely: even in February 1392, when, in a meeting of the Council at Westminster, it was proposed that Alexander Neville and Robert de Vere should be allowed to return home, and to be restored to their former state, both temporal lords and churchmen so vehemently resisted as to compel the king to reject the idea;[26] and no further opportunity presented itself, for soon they too died, Neville[27] in May following, De Vere[28] before the year was out (both at Louvain); and it was not until January 1397 that the judges exiled to Ireland by the 'Merciless Parliament' could be given leave to return to England.[29]

Notes

1　*Rot. Parl.*, III, 219–20.
2　According to Walsingham (*Chronicon Anglie, 1328–1388*, 372), Michael was to be fined 20,000 marks; according to Knighton (II, 221), he was ordered to surrender to the king, but 'ad relevamen communitatis regni', £12,000 which he had gained by holding up people's business until they had first paid him fines as a condition of his expediting it.
3　*Eulogium*, III, 360.
4　Op. cit., II, 236–7.
5　*Polychronicon*, IX, 104.
6　Ibid.; Knighton, II, 241.
7　*Chronicon Anglie*, 383.
8　*Rot. Parl.*, III, 229.
9　Ibid.
10　Ibid., 229–30.
11　*Report touching the Dignity of a Peer of the Realm* (London, 1820–9), IV, 725; 726–7.
12　*D.N.B.*, XX, 246.

13 Op. cit., II, 250. For a surprisingly long time Neville lay low in his diocese but, when attempting to cross overseas in a small boat, was captured off Tynemouth in mid-June 1388, then to be kept in custody by the mayor of Newcastle until 28 November when he escaped to the Low Countries (*Yorkshire Archaeological Journal*, XLVII, R. G. Davies, 'Alexander Neville, Archbishop of York, 1374–1388', 99–100.

14 Ibid., 251.

15 F. Devon, *Issues of the Exchequer Henry III–Henry VI* (London, 1837), 234.

16 *The Complete Peerage*, XII, Part I, 439–40.

17 For the following notice of process, see *Rot. Parl.*, III, 236–8.

18 The impeachment of the judges who had sealed the notorious *Questions* lasted from Monday, 2 March, until Friday, the 6th; and their trial was immediately (on the 6th) followed by that of Bishop Rushook of Chichester (the king's confessor), and soon (on the 12th) by that of Sir Simon de Burley (under-chamberlain), John, lord Beauchamp of Holt (steward of the Household), Sir John Salisbury and Sir James Berners (knights of the Chamber). The trial of the last-named four was resumed on 13 April (the first day after the break for Easter) and in the case of Burley lasted until 5 May, when he was condemned and beheaded near the Tower; on 12 May Beauchamp and Berners were condemned to be beheaded, and Salisbury to be drawn and hanged; and on the same day Bishop Rushook was sentenced to forfeiture, the disinheritance of his heirs, and, like the judges, to exile for life in Ireland.

19 Forfeited lands to the value of nearly £10,000 had been granted out in fee simple by midsummer 1389 (*E.H.R.*, LXXI, C. D. Ross, 'Forfeiture for Treason in the Reign of Richard II', 570–1).

20 *Rot. Parl.*, III, 245; *Complete Peerage*, XII, Part I, 441.

21 *Rot. Parl.*, III, 274; the petition was granted.

22 *Complete Peerage*, loc. cit.

23 *Rot. Parl.*, III, 668. In Henry IV's reign, and under Henry V, Michael the second earl would appear to have regularly attended parliament, but seems not to have made any special mark except as a soldier. According to the testimony of his son William, duke of Suffolk, at his trial for treason by impeachment in 1450, he served Henry IV 'in all the viages in his daies by See and Lande that were made oute of this lande, in the which he was at all' (ibid., V, 176), and certainly it was at Henry V's siege of Harfleur that he died (of dysentery) on 18 September 1415. His eldest son, Michael, who briefly succeeded him in the earldom, fell at Agincourt some five weeks later (25 October).

24 *Rot. Parl.*, III, 250.
25 *D.N.B.*, XVI, 33. Michael's body was evidently brought back to England at some point, for he was buried with his wife (who had died before October 1386) in the church of the Carthusians founded by the family at Hull (*Complete Peerage*, XII, Part I, 440).
26 *Polychronicon*, IX, 264.
27 *D.N.B.*, XV, 244. On 30 April 1388 (during the second session of the Merciless Parliament) Neville had been translated by Urban VI from York to the see of St Andrews, but, with Scotland in the obedience of the anti-pope, this move was illusory, and merely had the effect of deprivation. In exile he served as a parish priest at Louvain, where he died and, in the church of the Carmelites, was buried.
28 *D.N.B.*, XX, 246. Not long after seeking refuge in the Low Countries, De Vere and De la Pole had obtained a safe conduct from Charles VI of France and gone to live in Paris. It was after De la Pole's death that De Vere joined Neville in Louvain, where they lived together until the latter's death. De Vere died as the result of an accident in a boar-hunt. His embalmed body was brought back to England, for burial at Earl's Colne (Essex). But this was not until November 1395; and although Richard II, Archbishop Courtenay of Canterbury, and many other bishops and heads of monastic houses attended the exequies, only few from among the lay peers did so—'quia nondum digestum fuerat odium quod conceperant contra illum' (*Annales Ricardi Secundi*, in *Johannis de Trokelowe et Henrici de Blaneforde, Chronica et Annales*, ed. H. T. Riley, R.S., 1866, p. 185).
29 *Annales Ricardi Secundi*, p. 195.

Appendix

Michael de la Pole's own estates

Michael de la Pole did not succeed his father, William, in most of the family lands, until the latter's death in 1366. Understandably so. But even before then he had been well provided for. By 1354 he was holding the manor of Blyborough[1] in the parts of Lindsey in Lincolnshire, one of a chain of family estates close to the line of Ermine Street and within easy reach of the lower Trent. By then, too, he had Grassthorpe (Nottinghamshire),[2] on the west bank of the Trent below Newark. Already, down in Northamptonshire, he also held the manor of Grafton.[3]

Grafton was one of a parcel of eight manors which belonged to the alien priory of Wilmington (Sussex), a daughter house of the Norman abbey of Grestain, and were worth, as collectively assessed by the Exchequer in 1349, £86-odd a year.[4] First sequestrated by Edward III for the duration of the French war, they had been leased by the abbey to the Black Prince in settlement of the ransom of his prisoner, Jean de Melun, lord of Tancarville, the hereditary patron of Grestain, and then, in November 1348, conveyed by the prince, evidently in repayment of debts of his own, to Tidemann of Limburg, the receiver of the stannary of the duchy of Cornwall, who, long connected with William de la Pole as exporter and financier assisting the English war effort, demised them, some time between April 1350[5] and November 1354,[6] to three of William's sons. The youngest, Edmund, received Dornford (Cambridgeshire) and Creeting St Olave and Mickfield (Suffolk). Thomas obtained Norton under Hamdon (Somerset), Conock (Wiltshire), Ramridge (Hampshire) and Marsh Gibbon (Buckinghamshire). Michael at first acquired only Grafton. However, when Thomas died (October 1361), Michael inherited all his share,[7] continuing to hold these priory lands until, in 1379–80, he severally rented them for life to his four younger sons,[8] for each of whom, in 1384, he created an estate in tail,[9] having previously, while chancellor, liberated the lands from liability to clerical tenths.[10] Incidentally, it was on the basis of rents from the manors that, in 1373, Michael had covenanted for his daughter Anne's marriage.[11]

In the meantime, on 21 June 1366, nearly five months after Michael's first baronial summons to parliament, his father had died, leaving him most of the family's own property, much of it entailed. This property of Michael's was very considerable.[12] There were the estates in the parts of Lindsey, and so now, in addition to Blyborough, Michael held the manors of Firsby, Harpswell, Messingham, Appleby and, in the Isle of Axholme, Westwood. Farther north in Lincolnshire there was also property at Barton-on-Humber, on the south bank of the estuary directly opposite the port of Hull. On the north bank, both in and adjacent to the port, was quite the densest concentration of Michael's inherited properties: some fifty messuages in Hull itself, the manors of Myton-on-Humber and Sculcoates, and lands in Drypool, Hessle, North Ferriby, West Ella, Cottingham and Newland. Out to the east, in Holderness, close to Burstwick and its many members (once held by William de la Pole by royal grant but later surrendered) was the manor of Rimswell (held in dower by Michael's mother until her death in January 1382), together with land in East Halsham. Up the coast towards Flamborough was the manor of Bewholme. A morning's ride westwards from Hull was North Cave, and, twice as far again, on the near side of the great road to the north and not far from Pontefract, was an estate at Little Smeaton. Alongside that same road, too, only directly north by some twenty-five miles, was the manor of Cowthorpe, on the river Nidd, together with land at nearby Bickerton. Roughly another twenty-five miles farther north still, and once more close to the great road, was Sowber Hill (near Northallerton) in the wider valley of the Swale. Farther north again, at a similar distance and now beyond the river Tees, was a tight little huddle of manors—the Isle, Bradbury, and Preston-le-Skerne—all in the valley of the river Skerne, roughly half-way between Darlington and Durham. These Durham lands, when leased by the Exchequer after Michael's condemnation for treason in the 'Merciless Parliament' (1388), were to pay an annual rent of £29 6s 8d. By no means all his forfeited hereditary estates were then farmed out by the Exchequer, but the values of such *others* as were actually leased (and of which the farms happen to be known) amounted to an additional £200 per annum.[13]

To all these lands so far mentioned must be added the lands Michael held *jure uxoris*. Although it was probably in 1359,[14] certainly no later than within a year of Sir John de Wingfield's death in 1361,[15] that Michael had married Sir John's daughter and heir, Katherine, it was not until after the death of her mother (Eleanor) in 1375 that Michael came into possession of her inheritance. This, however, was again considerable. It comprised a compact group of estates in north-east Suffolk—the manors of Wingfield, Stradbrook, Syleham and Fressingfield—together with, and at no great distance, the manors of Huntingfield, Saxmundham and Sternfield, and, up in Norfolk, the manor of Saxlingham.[16] When these manors, albeit excluding Huntingfield and Saxmundham, were leased by the Exchequer in 1388, following their forfeiture, to Michael's son, Michael, and his brother, Edmund, their rentable value was assessed at 160 marks (£106-odd) per annum.[17] This figure raises the sum of the annual value of Michael's lands held by right of inheritance and marriage which were actually leased following his condemnation in 1388, and for farm rents which are actually known, to over £330. In this calculation, palpably based on only partial evidence, no account has been taken of such incidentals as the twelve shops Michael owned in the London parishes of St Mary Wolnoth and St Michael Cornhill,[18] the great inn in Lombard Street (once belonging to the Bardi) and another such inn at Stamford;[19] nor of the valuable lands he held on lease—the manors of Langham and Peldon (Essex) and Little Burley (Northamptonshire), of which he had the reversion[20]—and the manor of Castle Carlton (Lincolnshire).[21] Among other inestimables was his hereditary patronage of the priory of Thornholme (Lincolnshire).[22]

Michael also owned in Hull 'a goodly house of brick, like a palace, with fair orchards and gardens', together with three other houses, each with a brick tower, all four houses built by himself; and in London, near the Thames, he built another fine house.[23]

Notes

1 *Cal. Charter Rolls, 1344–1417*, 142; *Cal. of Inquisitions post mortem, Edward III*, XI, 139.
2 Grassthorpe, along with Blyborough and also Harpswell (Lincs.), Michael gave in 1383 to his heir, Michael, on the occasion of the latter's marriage to Katherine Stafford.
3 *CCR, 1354–60*, 659–60.
4 *CPR, 1348–50*, 442.
5 Ibid., 513. (In April 1350 Tidemann was given a royal licence to dispose of the Wilmington priory estates 'to any Englishman'.)
6 *CCR, 1354–60*, 659–60.
7 *Cal. Inqs. p.m., Edward III*, XI, 39.
8 *CPR, 1377–81*, 338, 526.
9 Ibid., *Ibid., 1381–85*, 374.
10 *CCR, 1381–85*, 388.
11 Ibid., *1369–74*, 555.
12 *Cal. Inqs. p.m., Edward III*, XII, 54–6; *Cal. Charter Rolls,*

1341–1417, 277; CCR, *1377–81*, 237; ibid., *1381–85*, 57, 494; CFR, *1383–91*, 251, 253, 255, 258, 281, 285, 288, 296; CPR, *1388–92*, 190, 196, 208–9, 242.

13 CFR, *1383–91*, 248–58, 281–96, *passim*.
14 CCR, *1354–60*, 636.
15 CPR, *1361–64*, *180*.
16 Cal. Inqs. p.m. *Edward III*, XIV, 232; CFR, *1368–77*, 296; CCR, *1374–77*, 159; CPR, 1381–85, 555; ibid., *1388–92*, 209.
17 CFR, *1383–91*, 261.
18 CCR, *1389–92*, 52–3.
19 CFR, *1383–91*, 224, 248.
20 CCR, *1377–81*, 236–7.
21 Cal. of Inquisitions Miscellaneous, IV, 190.
22 CCR, *1381–85*, 494.
23 D.N.B., XVI, 33.

Index

* See photograph of his Bolton Castle in Colin Platt: 1984. Medieval Britain ~~Englford~~ from the air; p. [143]
London: George Philip, 1984.